Rock Climbing

The Complete Rock Climbing Guide to Technique

(Complete Guide on How to Rock Climb for Beginners)

William Drolet

Published By **Oliver Leish**

William Drolet

All Rights Reserved

Rock Climbing: The Complete Rock Climbing Guide to Technique (Complete Guide on How to Rock Climb for Beginners)

ISBN 978-1-77485-480-8

No part of this guidebook shall be reproduced in any form without permission in writing from the publisher except in the case of brief quotations embodied in critical articles or reviews.

Legal & Disclaimer

The information contained in this ebook is not designed to replace or take the place of any form of medicine or professional medical advice. The information in this ebook has been provided for educational & entertainment purposes only.

The information contained in this book has been compiled from sources deemed reliable, and it is accurate to the best of the Author's knowledge; however, the Author cannot guarantee its accuracy and validity and cannot be held liable for any errors or omissions. Changes are periodically made to this book. You must consult your doctor or get professional medical advice before using any of the suggested remedies, techniques, or information in this book.

Upon using the information contained in this book, you agree to hold harmless the Author from and against any damages, costs, and expenses, including any legal fees potentially resulting from the application of any of the information provided by this guide. This disclaimer applies to any damages or injury caused by the use and application, whether directly or indirectly, of any advice or information presented, whether for breach of contract, tort, negligence, personal injury, criminal intent, or under any other cause of action.

You agree to accept all risks of using the information presented inside this book. You need to consult a professional medical practitioner in order to ensure you are both able and healthy enough to participate in this program.

TABLE OF CONTENTS

introduction 1

Chapter 1: Movement Is Climbing! 3

Chapter 2: Get Moving Your Feet! 10

Chapter 3: Grab A Grip! 20

Chapter 4: Learn Proper Body Positioning 31

Chapter 5: 10 Rock Climbing Essentials 36

Chapter 6: Belaying, Anchoring, Knotting And Belaying 46

Chapter 7: Strengthen The Climbing Warriors Within 55

Chapter 8: The Benefits Of Rock Climbing 62

Chapter 9: The Different Types Of Rock Climbing 68

Chapter 10: Climbing Gear 74

Chapter 11: Safety Tips 81

Chapter 12: The Different Types Of Faces 87

Chapter 13: Handholds And Grips 97

Chapter 14: Footwork Techniques 107

Chapter 15: What Makes Climbing Mountains Dangerous And Difficult? 114

Chapter 16: What Makes Climbing Mountains Costly? 145

Chapter 17: What Are The Benefits From Climbing
Mountains? 165
Conclusion 181

Introduction

This book outlines practical steps and methods on how you beginning to climb can improve your the techniques and skills of climbing and how to increase your progress by forming the right type of thought.

We were born with the ability to climb. It is a natural trait for humans, just like running and walking. It is a natural skill that we lose when we learn as children that climbing is risky. It was taught to us that risks of climbing can cause physical injuries. We should therefore avoid climbing and stay on the pavements where it's safer.

So , how do we achieve the ability to naturally return to the top?

The answer is much more simple than you imagine. We must learn to properly use our bodies. When we encounter terrain that is unfamiliar and are scared, it can be difficult for us. However, if we can let go of fearand walk our feet and hands over rocks and slopes, we will re-discover the thrill of adventure. We are able to regain our natural desire to return.

This is the essence of what this book is about. It's about learning and revisiting learning. It's about discovering and re-discovering of happiness in the ability to move, of focus on one's own excitement, of being free of distractions and focusing on the goal of achieving it!

Are you prepared to climb? Are you looking forward to it? You must be!

Thank you for buying this book. I hope you like it!

Chapter 1: Movement Is Climbing!

To climb, you must perform the proper movement. It is all about the body's movement over stones. It is crucial to be able to balance your body using both feet and hands.

Climbing is all about movement. We must understand the machinery of our body. We must understand the way it works and how to use it for the most effective climbing. As we encounter more rocks or slopes we are able to see how we can improve and where our weaknesses lie. Then we learn to adjust. We are taught how to compensate for our weaknesses. We learn to stay in control, and how to remain robust. We learn to be in the flow, and to be graceful and joyful.

For many one of the things that pops into their mind when they hear of rock climbing is safety equipment and gear. Of course, there's no harm in thinking about the safety first. Gravity is a fact in the end. It is important to be aware of the possibility of falling and its effects. But the fundamentals of climbing does not have anything to be attributed to specialized equipment. It all boils down to the act of moving.

That's why the first lesson we teach has to do with the ability. It starts with the basics, and the fundamentals require us to move our feet and hands. The climbing equipments are merely secondary considerations, but are equally important to support us during our climb. So let's get to it.

6 Essential Climbing Tips

The first step is general tips for climbing. Remember these general rules in mind. They can assist you in making effortless transitions, and climb more effectively and safely.

Be aware and consider your options before you move

It is important to keep the fact that rock climbing demands the mind just as it requires physical. Before you begin to tackle climbing, make sure you take a long glance at the rock's surface. Spend time looking at the cliff's surface. Find footholds and handholds. Find places to rest.

Do you notice the chalk markings? These are the marks that other climbers before you used. Be sure to look for scuff marks as well as footholds, too. It is crucial to consider your route before you attempt to climb to climb the rock. Find the most effective strategy to climb up.

Energy and effort is quickly wasted. Don't rely solely upon your strength. Instead, you need to conserve the most energy you can with your head. The most important thing is to keep your cool. Remain centered. This is the best method to solve all kinds of issues.

Be careful not to hug the rock.

So you love rock climbing, huh? This doesn't mean you need to take it in your arms. Hugging the rock is among of the most frequent errors that novices make. Keep in mind that there's no reason to get this close. Be careful not to lean into the stone's surface. Why is this a problem? It's because climbing is about moving and finding balance. If you are able to hug the rock, the weight moves from your legs to the ground. It makes it even more difficult to keep your balance.

To ensure the best balance, your body must be set at 90 degrees towards the surface of the earth. Your hips must be in a centered position throughout the day, with your feet resting on footholds to maintain stability. Your movements with your feet and hands must be in tune with the fundamental aim of ascending, while simultaneously maintaining your the right balance.

Put your trust in your feet.

The strength of the upper body is, of course, vital for climbers of all levels. But that doesn't mean you can only count on these muscles. In fact it is best to utilize your feet and legs to lift you up. Use footholds to lift your body instead of lifting your weight up using your arms and hands. Keep in mind that you should reserve muscles in your upper back for hanging and vertical routes , so when you are able, utilize your muscles on your feet and legs.

Use the three basic foot position.

There are three fundamental foot positions that you must master. These include toeing, edging, and smearing. Toeing, as the word suggests, is the use of your toes to hold to the heel. The opposite of this, edging is the use of both the outer and the inner edges of your shoes.

Smearing, in the end, is about placing as much can of your foot onto the rock. Make use of friction and use it effectively to hold your foot in the right position. We will discuss this in the future as we dive further into foot exercises.

Hold the rock in your hands.

While your feet and legs should be utilized to push and propel your arms and hands are to be utilized for assessing and pulling on different kinds of handholds. Also, your feet and hands must be working in sync. You'll encounter a variety of handholds. Utilize your hands to examine the surface of the rock, in the hope of locating the handholds that are the most efficient.

Make use of your hands to grab and hold. Be sure to be focused on finding the best and not just the most perfect. If you don't, you'll be stuck on the rocks for the rest of your life.

Be careful not to grip too in a tight way. The force of gripping too tightly requires a lot of strength. It eventually makes you weaker. If you're weak and weak, you will likely slide off. If you can it is recommended that you hold your handholds with ease. Be assured that you will be able to learn more about handholds and fingers grips in the future.

Be flexible and move in the direction of the flow!

Rock climbing is also a sport that involves the flow of movement and flow. This is why you must be careful not to climb in a jerky method. Think of it as an exercise in verticality. The most important thing to do is grace. A movement should flow into another. The movements should flow seamlessly. It is essential to make smooth transitions.

Grab the grip and grab the grip. Place your foot on the foothold and then push your body upwards. Keep your breathing steady. Relax. Use the big footholds and handholds, so you are able to rest. It is important to shake your hands and arms to keep your blood flowing. Remember, it's a dance, and you should join in with the rock!

Chapter 2: Get Moving Your Feet!

Our arms aren't designed to hold weight or helping us stay balanced. The arms and legs are designed to perform the task. If you're a climber, you must work as hard at learning the basics of solid footwork. Unfortunately, many climbers concentrate all their attention on the hand and they do not realize the importance for their legs.

We've covered the importance of keeping your in balance by using the feet. How can you increase the weight that rests on your feet and legs?

Look for the most suitable footholds.

Position the feet of your shoes in a specific way on the footholds.

Place your feet in a firm position and steady as you attempt for your body to move.

-Reinforce your weight over your feet and keep an upright body position.

Practice easy weight transfers between feet and legs while you climb.

Keep calm and remain calm and relaxed.

Do you know why climbers stumble and get tired easily? It's because they are focused on their hands and forget about their feet completely. This is why we have some suggestions to make the most of your feet while you climb.

Make sure you know your shoes.

Prior to anything else, it's vital to be in alignment to your footwear. Look at the picture below for guide.

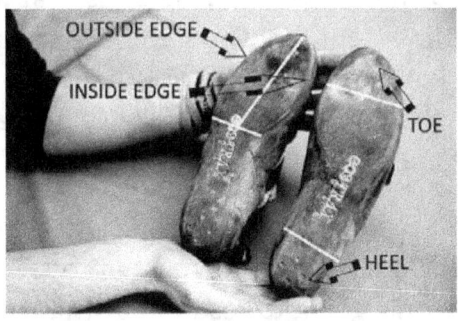

The parts of your shoes you wear will depend on the rock's direction and the form as well as the size of your foothold. In certain situations it is possible to use the toe. In other cases, the inside edge might be better. It is crucial that you are able to trust your shoes to hold the foothold. We'll go into more details about selecting the right climbing shoes in the future.

Your legs should be raised, but not down.

Sooner or later, you will realize enough that there isn't any perfect foothold. You will have to work with what you're given. But how do you tell which is the most effective? Each situation is different, however one of the basic rules is to stand on steps that are placed within your body.

Pick a foothold that is the knee to the shin as far as you can. Do not choose ones that are far to the side except for when you are steered or lying back. When you place your feet directly in front of the body you are giving yourself the chance to rest your weight on your feet.

Furthermore, you must be taking small steps at one time. Do not pressure yourself to take huge steps. It's only going to result in a strain on your body.

Avoid rock patches with dirt.

If you notice that the hold is covered with dirt or lichen, clean it up before you walk onto it. Prior to climbing it is also recommended to wash dirt and gravel off the bottom of your shoes. This will prevent you from sliding. Therefore, it is recommended to take a look at the hold prior to you place your feet onto it.

Strengthen your feet first.

Climbers who have experience are able to boast amazing foot strength. It is developed over years of practice as well as actual climbs. For a beginner, it is possible that you may not have the strength of your feet as you do. It is important to build it. The type of climbing shoes you choose is crucial.

Although experienced climbers may use less supportive shoes however, you should stick with rigid soled shoes for a beginner. Try to climb steadily. Don't rush the process. When you've finally achieved or increased your foot strength to be able to tackle more difficult climbing, you may opt for less supportive climbing shoes but be aware that this may require time.

Learn to master the footwork skills.

There are a variety of methods to get the most out of your feet in the climb. The most popular and easily mastered techniques used by novices are edging and smearing. This section will help you'll learn more about the other concepts for footwork that you could consider useful for developing your rock climbing skills. It is possible that you are not proficient in some of these methods yet, but at the very least, you need to be aware that you are able to use your feet in many different ways than you think of.

Edging

The art of edging is among the most important skills you should learn as climber. It is helpful when you come across smaller footholds. The footholds are small and do not let your entire shoe fit in it. There are two options. They can be used on the outside or inside part of the shoes.

The inside edge of the shoe is the portion of the shoe starting from the big toe downwards. The opposite edge is the portion of the shoe that runs from the pinky foot down. Edges are the method that is used when you focus on either the outside or inside edges of the climbing shoes to determine your balance or make sure you are ready to take the following step during your climb.

Edging and Outside Edging and outside Edging

So, which edge is better to use? The inside edge or the outside edge? The majority of climbers feel more comfortable using an inside edge. This is due to the fact that the bigger toe has more power to lift you up. There are instances however, where using an outside edge would be suitable.

For instance, if you're required for your body to be moved laterally across the surface of the rock, placing on the outer edge of your climbing shoes on the foothold is ideal. Since the pinky isn't as agile and weaker in general than the other ones, it isn't capable of holding your weight for a long time. If this is the situation, you must be more swift when using an outside edge.

In general, climbing shoes can be used to edge. However, the more robust shape, flat-shaped type is generally ideal for this technique of footwork. This is because the flat-shaped climbing shoes can absorb more pressure and easing the strain on feet that is caused by being on a tiny footrest.

Smearing

Do you think that footholds with small footprints can be a problem? Where do you place on your feet when it appears like there's no footholds? That's where the smearing method becomes a factor.

Smearing involves putting your shoe's sole against a slab or rock to provide support. It sounds scary when you consider it, but what makes this technique effective is friction. This is the reason you need to apply the maximum amount of pressure to crush your sole down into rock to keep your feet from sliding. It's like squashing bugs. In the amount pressure needed for smearing is contingent on the level of the terrain.

The most effective shoe to climb on is the one made of rubber. For this type of footwork you'll depend on friction. In that scenario, you'll like your shoes to have the most amount of rubber you can get. Since the pressure will be imposed on your toes, it is better off in flat shoes. Do not wear the type with a downturned sock. climbing shoes.

Hooking toe and Heel

For steeper and angled climbs, you must use more imagination. In these types of conditions, it is important to treat your feet as if they are your hands. In these scenarios toe and heel hooks are the best alternatives. Both allow you to remove weight from your hands while at the same time assist you in preparing for the next difficult move.

When the process of hooking toe and heel, pressure is essential. It is important to apply as as much pressure as possible on the rock, especially in case you are hooking to the next step.

Hooking your heel is accomplished by placing the heel of your foot on an anchor that is close to your waistline and occasionally higher. The only difference to hooking your toes is that you must utilize your toes or upper portion of your foot rather than. The heel hook is crucial for climbing a roof, islet or an arete.

When you perform this exercise it is necessary to utilize to the force of your hamstring to apply pressure. It is possible to do a heel hook using the edge of a jug or knob. By doing this type of exercises your hands and arms will be relieved of the weight, so you can shake off the excess weight or rest for a while until you're ready take the next step. It's also possible to utilize an heel hook in order to pull your body upwards.

You can also use toe hooking in lieu of heel hooking. It functions in the same manner, however pressure is applied to the your foot's top instead. A toe hook can be useful to keep you as near to your rock as is possible.

Certain climbing shoes are more suitable to hook over other shoes. If you're more suited to hooking your heel, it's recommended to select a shoe that has enough rubber around the heel. For those who prefer hooks on the contrary hand, you need to choose the shoe that has more toe patching made of rubber.

Flagging

This method is helpful in stopping your body from moving out to the side and falling. It requires one leg pointed in an opposite direction from the rest of your body with the primary goal of keeping your stability. This means that the leg that is extended is not intended to support you. It is used to move your balance. Check out the following images.

The Standard Flag The Standard Flag, Outside Flag and Inside Flag

The other leg is extended , either suspended or resting upon a rung in which case the climber may lose balance. Standard flags are most simple to master and is the first thing beginners typically learn to master.

Stemming

Have you ever made splits? It could be beneficial for rock climbing. This technique will require the least amount of strength, but takes the time needed to become proficient. To make this technique perform, you have to utilize the tension in your body to make it climb while pushing on the holds. Stemming can be very beneficial for climbers when climbing inside corners or in dihedrals. Stemming can also be a good chance for climbers rest for a while and shake their hands and arms.

Back Stepping

For beginners, they rely on a typical step that requires them to rotate their legs to make their hips are facing the rock's surface. If you are able to position the foot of one on a step in a way that your outside and not an inside hip faces towards the rock and your torso is lengthened, which will allow you to have an extended reach in the same direction . The other foot is in an erect position to ensure security and stability. This is known as back to stepping.

In this picture the woman is climbing with her left foot stepping back with her right one is flagging. This position lets her climb higher using one arm.

Don't let these strategies overpower you.

They seem quite difficult. They all require flexibility. You'll be able to master these skills by gaining flexibility first. Take your time to practice the exercises along with a stretching routine.

Chapter 3: Grab A Grip!

Alongside handhold techniques, footwork is important in rock climbing. Your feet and hands must be coordinated. Attention to your feet doesn't mean that you completely ignore your hands. Both require attention.

We'll be explaining the various types of grips you might be faced with, the best way to hold them more effectively using appropriate handhold techniques, and ways to improve your grip strength and overall strength. The chapter will begin with some suggestions.

Beware of over-gripping.

If the climb gets steeper than it gets steeper and higher, it is scary. Fear can lead to grab too much. This can cause a major issue. The over-gripping can cause an intense pump. It's extremely difficult for you to get back from it. It takes away strength. It can make climbers lose focus on the technique. It causes climbers to fall off the track.

Don't force yourself to grip too tightly on the grip. If you can you can use lightly grips. Keep in mind that you've got your feet to support you. Therefore, you don't need to bear the weight on your shoulders.

Know which direction to pull.

The ability to lower yourself naturally comes naturally for us. It's like climbing the ladder. However, it is not always possible to use the downward pull during rock climbing. In certain situations it is recommended to pull either in the opposite direction or up.

The side-pulling method is preferred when climbing a rock that is steep and has a the orientation of a sideways. When you pull toward the opposite direction, you will keep the weight of your feet on them and conserve your upper body strength. An upward or undercling pull however is ideal for when you must reach out for a hold that is far away. It can take time to master the best way to pull but, with the practice, you'll master this technique by instinct.

Maintain the arms straight.

If you're climbing up a steep rock, you should avoid bending your elbows. Your arms must be straight. This will prevent straining your biceps. By extending your arms you're hanging from the bone instead , which gives you more support. The elbows are not bending, however, it is not a choice when you are ready to start a workout. Be quick however. It's not a good idea to deplete the strength of your biceps in a short time.

Don't overextend your arms.

To grasp an unattainable grasp, there's the tendency to reach too far. Know that your reach has limits. Keep in mind that you must have a balance to keep. You're fighting against gravity. If you attempt to reach out too far you might lose a grasp on the feet, which increases the chance of falling. Instead of extending your arms too far and reaching out too far, you should try moving your feet upwards. First, moving your feet upwards lets you extend further and higher using your arms.

Learn how to handle different kinds of grips.

There are many methods of gripping rocks. Similar to feet, your grip must depend on the rock's position shape, size and shape.

Edges

They're probably the most popular type of holds for climbing on rocks. They are a horizontally-shaped handhold that has an outside edge that is positive. Certain edges can also be round. Some edges are smooth, but some have the lip that lets climbers pull off on the edges.

The widths of edges can vary. Some are narrow while others have enough width to accommodate the entire hand. The big edges are often referred to as buckets or jugs. Jugs are ideal for those who have yet to build an effective grip. They can be helpful when climbing overhanging rocks. One of the primary methods to grip edges is by crimping grip.

Crimping

Crimping gives you a firm hold on edges. The fingers' tips have a flat edges with the tips arched up over them. Be cautious when you use this kind of grip. If you squeeze too much, you could end up damaging the finger's tendons. If this happens you'll have to endure some time off. It could take a few several months before you recuperate from an injury.

Slopers

They are handholds that are rounded and are commonly used in slab climbs. As opposed to edges, slopers will not have the lip or positive edge which you can wrap the fingers. Instead of relying on a solid grip, slopers need skin friction with the surface of the rock.

Open Hand Grip

The open hand grip is perfect for grips that have sloping edges. It is recommended to use this grip when you are able to count on skin-to-skin friction. Although it might not be as sturdy as a crimp but the open hand grip is similarly strong, particularly when you use a chalk. The friction increases when chalk is placed over your fingertips.

This grip type takes patience to learn. If you come across this type of handhold try using your fingers to get a great sense of it. This will allow you to determine the right portion to grip. Some slopers have bumps or a small ridge, which lets climbers use a more secure grip. Once you've figured out the best thing to hold on to, start attaching your hands to the handhold, keeping your fingers in place. Press your thumb against a bump , if your sloper has one.

Pins

If edges are protruding, they form crystals or tiny knobs on the surface of rocks. These are referred to as pinches. The majority of pinches are tiny and difficult to perform. The most effective way to grab them is to use using the grip of a pinch.

Pinch Grips are based on the dimensions of the handhold.

Use a pinch grip simply pinching the handhold by placing your the thumb on one side and using the rest of the fingers to one side. The pinching is small and requires your thumb and fingers to be in close proximity. Put your middle and index fingers against your thumb. This makes the pinch grip feel more secure.

Pockets

There are also pockets in the surface of the rock and you could make use of them as handholds too. These are known as pockets. They come in a variety of dimensions and designs. Some permit climbers to place up to four fingers inside, while others are small enough that just one finger will fit inside the hole. Certain pockets are oblong-shaped and some are flat. Some pockets have deep ones as well as others with shallow pockets.

If you do come across pockets, make sure you examine it thoroughly by placing as many fingers as you can comfortably into the opening. Take a look inside. If you see dimples or lips in the pocket and you can use your fingers for pull on them. If the pocket can only accommodate only one or two fingers it is advised that you utilize your strongest fingers which could be the index or middle finger, or both, if the pocket permits it.

Sidepulls

An angled vertically or diagonally edge is often referred to as a sidepull. The name itself implies it is an edge that is located on your side , not over you. The handhold is designed to be pulled sideways , not straight down. If you are grabbing the sidepull, you must to resist the force of gravity by stretching your hands and feet to the opposite side.

The opposing forces are responsible for making sure your body is balanced and in a stable position. You can also rotate your hips and lean against the wall when the position an outside part of the shoes on the foothold. As one hand extends using a sidepull, towards the reverse direction you are able to extend further with the other hand.

Gastons

This kind of handhold is similar to the sidepull because they're both horizontally or vertically aligned. While the sidepull is situated to your left and the gaston is to your left, it's an handhold you'll discover right in front of you.

You can grasp this handhold with your fingers and palms while your thumb is pointed downwards. Your elbows should be bent. Make use of both hands pull away from you as if were trying to unlock the door of a sliding slide. This method is most effective if your feet are placed in a manner that they are able to resist the force pulling from your hands. Gaston is a tough method, but you can benefit from it on a variety of methods. It is important to master and practice the technique.

Underclings

This handhold is secured by the bottom. Utilize your fingers to grab the edge on the outside of the handhold. They come in a variety of dimensions and shapes. They can be in the shape of pockets, flakes or inverted edges, as well as cracks on the horizontal or diagonal. As with sidepulls and gastons these handholds require body tension. Your feet and hands must be placed in opposing directions in order to achieve the balance.

Hold the hold with the palm of your hand facing upwards while your thumb is pointed towards the outside. As you raise your hand, pull away from the hold and put your feet down on the ground underneath in the other direction. You may also grasp the hold using your thumb under it, and your fingers placed resting on the grips above.

Handholds that work well are if you hold them close to your mid-section. The further away it is from your mid-section, the more tension you'll feel, and the higher the chance that you'll fall off balance. Since these holds are very difficult, it is advised that you straighten the arms. When your arms are straight you will experience less strain.

Palming

What happens if there's no handholds? Do you have the ability to climb? If there aren't any holds that you can grab on to and you are able to use hands instead. Use your open hand. The skin-to-rock friction by pressing the heel of your palm against the rock surface will help to lift your body upwards. This method will also conserve your strength in your arms. You can push with your palm instead of lifting your weight by using your hands and arm.

It is likely that the surface of the rock isn't flat. There will be an irregularity there. Your palm should be towards the rock and then press your heel against the rock. The body weight will shift from the foot towards your palm. This gives you an chance to lift your feet. Be sure to maintain your equilibrium. Your other arm and leg should be positioned against the other side in order to complete this task.

Matching Hands

This is just about placing the hands of both hands close to one another. It is much easier to do using a wide edge. The handhold technique allows climbers to switch hands in order to be higher off on the next hold. The difficulty comes when you're dealing with a relatively thin edge.

The technique is feasible, but it's more complicated. If you want to do this, use your fingers rather than the entire hand. Begin by freeing each finger one at a stretch with one hand so that you are able to grasp a handhold that is higher.

It is important to strengthen your feet and your upper body to enhance your climbing skills. It is possible to practice these handhold techniques by doing indoor climbing on walls. Certain handholds are more difficult in their learning than others. Over years, the body will become more familiar with the movements until it becomes a part of muscles memory.

Chapter 4: Learn Proper Body Positioning

Now you know how to utilize your feet and hands and how to correctly put them on the supports to climb with more efficiency. However, you must learn another thing about your most valuable tool that is your body. To ensure that you are steady on the rocks while putting in less effort and energy You must also be aware of the proper posture of your body.

Be aware that there are a variety of ways to position your feet, hands and your body against the rock. The most important thing is to find the most effective method to position them so that you can maintain your balance.

How do you maintain your equilibrium?

We've spoken about the necessity of maintaining balance and stability. What is it exactly and how can you locate it? The point of gravity of your body is situated in the navel area. You should aim to keep this area in the middle between all the points of contact with the wall. When you're conscious about your centre, you'll be much better at determining the most effective methods to position your body in a way that the majority of your weight is on your feet, not your hands and arms.

Although you might have an impressive upper body however, your forearms were not made to support the entire weight. Actually, they are one of the weakest links. Your legs are strong, which is the reason you must be aware of using them to the maximum extent possible.

When you climb to the top, you're in constant conflict with gravity. It's impossible to escape gravity. It will pull your down if you allow it to. You're given a vital tool , however. You can utilize your entire body to get around the obstruction.

We will review the correct body positioning based on the orientation of a rock. Be aware that you must be in alignment with gravity. It is not a good idea to work against gravity, therefore pay attention.

How do you position your body's body against vertical walls?

If you are on a wall that is vertical your feet will be perpendicular to ground. It is possible to put the majority all of the load on your feet putting your body near to your wall is possible. This can be accomplished by moving your hips close to the wall.

If your pull off your hips from the wall you'll notice that your body weight is shifting from the feet onto your arms. This isn't ideal since you're working against gravity. You want to be in alignment with gravity. Keep your hips in a tight position. Keep this in mind when you climb and take each step, just as the climber in the picture below.

How do you position your body to the slab?

There is a pull on gravity goes straight downwards in the event that your body's parallel to the ground. The angle of the rock's surface shifts, it's important that your body's position is adjusted in line with the changes. When you walk on a slab, for example you'll encounter tiny handholds. You will need to apply smearing techniques. In this scenario your feet are already absorbing a lot of the load and your arms are sole purpose of assistance and to balance.

As long as you keep your hips close to wall when is possible is a good idea for the vertical wall, this position is not ideal for the slab. This is among the numerous mistakes climbers make. Don't allow yourself to fall into the same trap.

The climber is being pulled down by gravity around 90 degrees. In this case, putting her body in 90 degrees will be the most effective method of climbing. Why? With her hips a distance from her wall, the feet carry the all of the weight. In this position she lets her lower part to push straight downwards as she climbs using her arms, and then move her feet in tandem with it.

This body position will also increase the amount of surface that gets which her feet are covering upon the floor. It also gives the feet more grip, which is crucial in spreading. By placing her body in this manner it allows gravity to work by letting gravity pull her towards the wall.

How do you position your body to be on an overhang?

Overhangs can be tricky. When you have this type of rock's orientation it is important to anticipate your arms to carry greater weight. This is the time to use all of the upper-body strength to work. However, this doesn't mean that your entire weight must be carried through your arms. There's still a way to reduce the tension and not work with your pull on gravity. We can use this image as a an example.

The arm of the climber hang off the hold. Her hips are right next to the rock, and she isn't letting the feet roll off. She holds them to the footrest. Do you know what is likely to occur if she bends her elbows, or let her hips slump or leave her feet hang? She'll be prone to falling quickly.

The elbows that are bent will create more tension in the region that is able to only handle a certain amount of stress. If she allows her hips to drift away towards the wall she'll lose the hold of her feet. She'll slip off. In this situation it is best to use a heel hook. the best.

There's more to this however. To climb overhangs, climbers require more than just upper body strength. It requires strong core strength and an effective technique. It also requires plenty of time for training.

Make sure you warm up correctly.

When you're up against the wall in a strenuous climb, you'll be more difficult to stay aware of how your body is positioned. This is why it's essential to practice proper posture during warm-up.

You can always count on your strength to complete the climb but there is always a better way to tackle the climb. It is possible to climb easier. It is possible to make it less difficult. The more time you set aside to practice and warm up to warm up, the faster it becomes an automatic process for you. Additionally it is vital to strengthen your core for climbing as well. It can be beneficial to incorporate certain core strength exercises in your warm-up.

Chapter 5: 10 Rock Climbing Essentials
Climbing isn't an expensive pastime. The exhilarating experience of climbing is worth every penny. It is possible to take advantage of your buddy's spare shoes and use equipments together. If you're committed to this it is essential to spend more in your development.

Improvement involves purchasing the necessary equipment.

Climbing Shoes

Your feet are vital tools that you should increase the value of your feet when climbing with the appropriate pair of footwear. Climbing shoes consist of rubber soles that are sticky. This makes it possible for climbers to get the most of friction. They're flexible and comfortable enough to support and safeguard your feet while at the same time.

Find the shoes for climbing that fit snugly. They can be worn with socks. There are three different types of climbing shoes that you have to be aware of. They include slip-ons, Velcro and lace-up. If you like long climbs, shoes with lace-ups are the best choice because they're not easily removed. If you're looking for quick climbs such as sport and boulder climbing, however, the other two designs are the best.

The climbing shoe you need to wear will vary. For beginning climbers, you will need select a pair that is comfortable to walk around. In this stage you should concentrate on easy climbing. No complicated foot placements are yet. As you progress from one level one after the other, you may require a change to climbing shoes that are more snugly fitted. Toes that are down-turned are uncomfortable, but they can be extremely useful for climbers who want to tackle difficult technical routes.

Chalk

Another important aspect of climbing to remember is chalk. Climbing chalk is made from magnesium carbonate. The same kind is used by gymnasts. It is necessary to keep your hands from scratching and chafing on the rock surface. It is also necessary for greater grip on handholds.

Climbing chalk comes in different forms. Although loose chalk can be useful but block chalks are more affordable. Chalk balls are also readily available. You can make use of them by shaking them with your fingers. Pick the one that suits your preferences.

Chalk Bag

If you're using chalk, you'll require bags to store it in. There's nothing complicated about this crucial piece of climbing equipment. Like chalk, you're able to choose one that you are comfortable with , as you can ensure that the bag has a sturdy waist belt and reliable buckle. The opening on the top is designed to comfortably accommodate your hand when you reach to grab some chalk.

Carabiners

Oft known as "biners" These are loops made of metal with an opening through which rope and webbing can go through. The gate is able to be closed by closing it, creating a secure closed loop. Carabiners were originally constructed from steel, but modern versions are made from high-quality aluminum.

There are many kinds that you can pick from. Certain are equipped with keys-lock gates, while others feature wire gates. Since the rope is less likely to fall on its face the key lock type is the best option. Check the carabiners prior to you purchase them. Examine for wear and wear and tear. In addition, verify that the gate closes and opens smoothly.

Locking Carabiners

The main difference between a locking carabiners and normal carabiner is that the latter have a locking gate and cover. This is crucial for climbers of all levels. It is a vital component for completing your belay device and can be a part of the toprope system. Make sure you inspect the equipment thoroughly prior to making a purchase. For your own safety it is possible to select a model that will perform well in different environments.

Harness

Harnesses for climbing are created of a strong system made of loops of webbing. It is wrapped between the legs as well as the waist to provide optimal support. The harness comes with buckles of steel to attach. The loop is designed to attach devices for belay. It is also a great option to carry equipment.

A harness is extremely lightweight and thin but is extremely strong and durable. Since a harness is one of the most important tools that make up the safety of climbing it is vital that you invest in the best quality. Don't compromise on an appropriate harness.

It is highly recommended that you purchase a new one. While you're in the store try it out for a ride. While comfort isn't an issue with climbing shoes, it is a consideration for harnesses. Keep in mind that you'll wear it all the time while climbing and should feel at ease and supported by the harness.

It is also advisable to pick a bike with four gear loops along the belt. This isn't necessary to top-rope, but in the event that you want to move up to trad or sport climbing, you'll require it. By investing a bit more now, you can save you the hassle of purchasing a new one in the future. The price of climbing harnesses can vary, but the best quality ones can be priced at as low as $60.

Belay Device

Both the climber as well as the belayer are in sync. The belay device is connected to the harness of the belayer, which lets the belayer regulate the rope's movement. When the belayer shuts the device the rope is blocked from being able to escape. This is crucial to ensure the security that the climber. Belay devices can prevent the possibility of a catastrophic fall.

Belay Devices

Belay systems of today are built of aluminum. They are attached to the belayer's device via the carabiner. There are numerous types and brands to pick from. The most basic is Black Diamond ATC. Mammut, Trango, Metolius and Black Diamond ATC are designed with teeth, which makes it very simple to lock. The top belay systems that auto-lock in available include Trango Cinch and Petzl Grigri 2.

Dynamic Rope

For climbers it is your lifeline. Dynamic ropes are constructed from polymers that have been engineered to stretch to create thinner fibers. They consist of two elements of the kern as well as the mantle. The Kern is the rope's central part comprised of long, elastic, and durable fibers. The mantle, on the other hand is placed around the core, which is designed to protect it while at the same time help it to be easier to handle.

Since it's important enough and crucial, there are a variety of factors to take into consideration when purchasing an elastic rope. In the beginning, you must consider the length and the diameter. The typical length of rope will be 50 meters. But, it could be not enough for rappels or sport routes. To ensure that you're in good shape it is recommended to buy a bigger one. 60 meters might be enough, especially if you're just contemplating purchasing one.

Then, you must think about whether you would prefer the more costly dry treated type. A rope that is not treated dry is more likely to break down in the presence of water and humidity. It can also be difficult to use in wet conditions. If you use dry treated ropes, you'll be able to avoid these problems. The downside is the fact that the dried treated type is more costly.

Thirdly, it is important to consider the size of your rope. The ideal rope diameter is based on the type of climbing you like. For example, a lively rope that measures 8.9 up to 9.4mm of diameter would be great for long climbs on trads. However an elongated rope of 9.5 to 10.5 millimeters in diameter is ideal for sport and traditional climbing, and top-roping.

Ropes with thinner diameters are heavier and could be more difficult to maneuver by using belay devices. The thinner ropes weigh less, and more manageable. But they're more dangerous.

A top quality, flexible rope could cost as little as $120. Like harnesses, you should don't buy ropes that are used. Additionally, you must keep an eye on your rope for any damages. Ideally, they'll last for three years before they need to be replaced, but should the rope exhibit indications of wear and tear then it's time to get it replaced.

Quick Draws

It's essentially a pair of two carabiners joined through what is known as the dogbone. This dogbone is used to stop the carabiners from turning. Quick draws are very helpful for attaching bolts as well as for creating top-rope anchors.

Webbing

This is vital to anchor the toprope system. The boulders and trees can act as anchors. Webbing is what is used to anchor these anchors. In contrast to a dynamic rope webbing isn't as costly. It is available in various lengths. In the beginning, you might prefer webbing that has 1726-, 51-foot sections.

Chapter 6: Belaying, Anchoring, Knotting And Belaying

Now you are able to move your hands, feet and your body. You are aware of how to choose the right equipment. In this article, we'll go into the use of these tools for your security.

Understanding the Fundamental Concepts of the Standard Anchor

The whole climbing safety system is dependent entirely on anchors. That's why this is so crucial. This is the reason why it is highly recommended to seek out a professional for advice on this. This guideline is designed to aid you in understanding the basics of the subject and does not constitute a comprehensive guide.

There are some basic items you should be aware of prior to setting up an anchor. These principles comprise the following.

Only use SOLID ANCHORS.

As we mentioned earlier it is possible to use the tree or a rock to anchor. It must be strong and stable. Do not trust an anchor that can snap easily as dead twigs. You must find strong places to connect. This is the reason you require additional webbing so that you can establish an anchor with strength regardless of whether it is further from the site.

REDUNDANCY is essential.

Always consider anchors that are secure. It is essential to have at least 2 points for connection. In the event that one of them fails, have another.

Make sure you have the right anchors.

In the event that you're using more than one anchor it is important to ensure that the load is distributed equally between the anchors. This will ensure that your fall is secured and your weight supported while you fall.

There is no extension permitted.

A gap in the connecting points could be hazardous to the climber since it increases the stress on the anchor. We'll talk about limiting extensions in the near future, using the appropriate type of knots.

Beware of small angles.

The ideal angle is to not be more than 60 degrees. The ideal angle is an angle of 20 degrees. Angles that are wider can result in greater forces, which is something you would not like to occur.

For a better understanding of these guidelines, you should think SARENE-SA.

Use solid anchors

Make it redundant

Be sure that it's Equalized

Do not allow extensions.

Make use of small angles

This acronym could save your life or someone else's!

Understanding the Basic Knots

We will go over four fundamental knots in this article and their application. This is enough for anyone who is just beginning to get started.

Figure 8

It is one of the easiest knots to tie, and the strongest, Figure 8 can be used to secure the harness. It is also a great way to tie a second closed loop to a tree's trunk. See the photo below to learn the steps to tie the knot.

How do you make the Figure 8 knot on a Bight

This Figure 8 in a bight is ideal since it is likely that you will attach a carabiner to it and you will require the hole in order to make it possible. Make sure to pull as tight that you are able to.

Girth Hitch

This knot is extremely efficient in setting anchors, especially when you're using an anchor that is natural. It's also great to join two loops. The greatest benefit of Girth Hitch Girth Hitch is that they're quick and easy to create. Also, it puts less stress on the webbing or rope.

It is essential to connect using the strongest and thin area in the structure. In the illustration below the portion that is just above the root of the tree would be the most suitable. What is the significance of this? Should you tie the webbing on the thickest point you can expect it to slide down to the smaller regions when pulled hard. If you place it at the thinnest point it is less likely of it sliding, which implies a safer as well as more secure to the webbing.

Clove Hitch

As with the Girth Hitch like the Girth Hitch Clove Hitch can also be used for constructing anchors. It is possible to use this knot for attaching objects to the rope's center and also to connect yourself using your harness to anchor. Another possible use of the Clove Hitch can be used for creating a carabiner block which can be used to create a single rope rappel. This is a great option for climbers for securing themselves when they climb to the summit of a climb instead of using an anchor for their personal.

This is how to make the Clove Hitch.

How do you create an Clove Hitch

Munter Hitch

This is among the most flexible knots, and is also fairly basic. The majority of climbers use this knot to rappel. It is also used as a backup method so that climbers are secure on long climbs in the event that they lose or lose their device for belaying.
In some instances it is possible that in some cases, the Munter Hitch may also be utilized as a substitute to belay devices, however it is not recommended. Utilizing the rope to do this could be secure for the climber however, not

the rope since it could cause severe injury and cause excessive wear on the rope.

It is possible to refer to the below image for how to make a Munter Hook.

How do you create a Munter Hitch

How do you get a Munter Hitch

In the meantime, you are able to make these knots to suit your specific needs. When you begin climbing more frequently and get deeper more deeply into the world of rock climbing and the climbing world, you'll be able to discover new ways to tie your rope.
Basics of Belaying

Belaying is among the most important skills you have learn before you put your hand onto the rock. To be a successful climber, it is essential to be a competent belayer first. As belayers is responsible for the safety of the climber is your obligation. We refer to the rope as the climber's lifeline as should the climber fall the burden shifts to his rope from the rocks. The job of belayer is to stop the fall. You can accomplish this by severing the rope.

It is your responsibility to make sure that everything from knots, to the harness and the entire belay system is installed. Make sure to keep an eye on the harness as well as that on your climber.

In this segment you will learn to set up the top rope belay.

Install the belay.

The first step to do is install your belay system. The method of feeding the rope that is dynamic into the device differs from one brand to the next. Follow the steps in the instruction manual. Once the rope has been inserted into the device for belay, connect the locking carabiner to the loop and then the rope. Then, you can attach the harness to the carabiner that locks and secure it. You must ensure that everything is secured.

How do you make the belay

Try the active posture.

Be aware that, as belayer, you're giving support to your climber. Set your legs apart at the shoulder width. Be sure that your body is balanced and your feet are steady and solidly placed to the earth.

Place yourself where you can clearly see your climber as well as the route that he or she is following. It is best when you place yourself near the rock. By staying close to the rock's surface it will decrease the distance that is necessary for falling.

Choose the hand to use with the brake.

The dominant hand is employed as brakes, while the other hand acts as a guide. See the picture below for the correct hand placement onto the rope.

Your hands should be at the top of the rope at all times while you monitor the climber. The image below will show you how to manage the rope's slack when the climber is climbing to the top.

The rope should be pulled on using your hand as a guide. With the brake hand off of the rope, pull off the rope to your hips. Make sure that your hand is prepared to stop at all times.

If the climber has the ability to descend then follow the steps below, from images 4 , 6 and 7. You must create an slack as soon as possible so that your climber is able to come down. The rope should be fed to the belay system, from your brake hand and then into the guide hand. To ensure that the climber is able to make a safe landing, cut the rope from time to the.

Review the safety guidelines.

When the climber and belayer just a few feet from one another A simple safety script must be followed to facilitate understanding and to facilitate communication. The safety guidelines are in this manner.

Climber: "ON BELAY?"

The climber inquires of the belayer whether or not the equipment in the belay system has been securely connected.

Belayer: "BELAY ON."

The belayer should assure climbingers that their belay equipment is prepared and that they are prepared to cut the rope in the event an accident occurs.

Climber: "CLIMBING."

The climber is all set for the start of his climb. He or she puts his or her life in the shoulders of the belayer immediately.

Belayer: "CLIMB ON."

The belayer offers the climber a thumbs up.

If the climber is prepared to descend, he or she must shout, "DOWN." The belayer will ensure that the rope is in good shape and does not have any looseness. The belayer should then instruct the climber to get their hands off of the rock's surface. Then , the belayer will guide the rope to ensure that the climber is ready to start the rappel.

Chapter 7: Strengthen The Climbing Warriors Within

"You will only go the height that your mind allows." ~ Robyn Erbesfield

Climbing isn't only about stamina or strength. It's not only about moving. It's definitely physically demanding. However, it's just as challenging as a mental challenge physically demanding.

If you don't have the right mindset, the proper attitude as well as the motivation to make the next step and the drive to continue and the determination to complete physical strength will matter just a bit less. If you're facing an uphill climb and you are in a hurry, you must be focused. It is important to stay at peace and calm. It is important to be able to relax so that you can focus on your task. This isn't going to happen if you do not possess a warrior's mindset.

The strength of your mind is as vital in the same way as strength and endurance of your body. This is why we are taking this time to improve how you think.

Do not attach your self-image with your performance.

This is the fate of many. It is painful to be forced to put in the effort, put in the effort and time but not get the results you had hoped for.

But , you must accept that you, or anyone else isn't able to do everything flawlessly every time. It's not necessary to. Your best effort is sufficient.

Your accomplishments do not determine your value as an individual. Remove your self-image from your performance. Concentrate on the learning process and the possibility of growing rather than on the final result. It will also lessen the most common cause of frustration. It can also make it easier to have fun climbing, in the way it should be, at its core, a pleasure to be appreciated.

Release yourself from the chains that tie your sense of self-worth to the sport you choose. It's an empowering experience. It eases anxiety and pressure. When you're free of the negative thoughts and emotions You will be able to be able to climb more easily. You'll climb more easily. You will be able to climb higher and more joyfully!

You can surround yourself with positivity.

Negativity can be draining. It can be emotionally, mentally and physically demanding. Keep in mind that our actions and thoughts influence the actions of others. The actions and thoughts of others also affect us. If you're hanging out with similarly frustrated people who complain about everything, you're likely to bear that burden negative energy. It is a downward pull of this negative energy is greater than the downward pull of gravity.

What you require is positive vibe. Pick your climbing partners carefully. You should surround yourself with positive motivated, positive people. Positive energy can be just as infectious as negative one. It can bring you to enjoy a great deal of pleasure. The gift of their motivational words and attitudes can have a massive impact on the development of your capabilities and techniques.

Prepare yourself to leave your comfortable zone.

When climbing, it's about doing as much as you can , even when it causes physical discomfort. It's about forcing your body to endure even more. It is possible to endure more if you're mentally prepared. Being mentally prepared is putting your fears aside and focusing on the seemingly impossible to achieve, is even possible!

The fact that you're typically on this kind of thinking doesn't necessarily mean that it's good for you. Sometimes all you need to do is entertain the idea that you are able to achieve more, and that you're capable of greater things in order to turn it a reality.

Understand, assess and manage the risk.

The limit of your comfort zone should not mean that you can completely eliminate your fears. A healthy amount of anxiety is beneficial. It can make you cautious, but not too cautious. It stops you from taking risks that are not necessary.

You must realize that the effort of pushing your body to perform more can be risky. In an activity as hazardous as climbing, it is important to be realistic and not be negative. It is essential to set the right expectations and not limit your capabilities. It is important to be neutral.

Be aware of the dangers that are involved. If you are aware of them then you're better able to make the situation less dangerous. It is possible to have safety measures in place. The key is preparation.

Develop your confidence.

Self-confidence is a function of self-image. If your self-image is deteriorating and your confidence declines, so does it. Worrying about your performance as a failure and negative phrases like "I don't" or "can't" can make your confidence wane.

Make a 180-degree turn. Place the past back where it is. Let it go once you've learned beneficial lessons. Use the valuable lessons to make use of them for self-improvement. What was I doing wrong on this climb? What method could I have employed to achieve a better result? What can I do to improve my technique so I can be more successful next time?

Make sure you focus on the things you manage. This is your progress. Make sure you focus on the things you can accomplish. Do not dwell on what could have happened that doesn't translate into anything productive.

Use visualization.

Instead of dwelling on the past and your mistakes Instead of dwelling on past mistakes and poor performances, why not go back to what you were able to do well. Make a point of imagining and reliving the moments over and over whenever you feel the negative thoughts getting into your life. Reliving these amazing moments The exhilarating sensation, the rush of joy and excitement that is flowing through your body, creates an optimistic ball of energy that can help you get yourself back on track from the past resentments.

Enjoy your wins regardless of how small they might seem. They're proof that you're doing things correctly. This is the time to let your confidence be elevated. A greater sense of confidence can go an extremely long way in the future of your endeavors.

Love climbing without reservation.

Don't love climbing to get there. Enjoy it regardless of the bruises and cuts as well as the frustrations, difficulties, the sweat, and tears. Happiness is for those who love without expectation, without limitations with no barriers or boundaries. Feel free to love. Enjoy your climb!

Chapter 8: The Benefits Of Rock Climbing

Rock climbing is a fantastic method to enjoy doing some exercise and exploring the outdoor. There are plenty of advantages to rock climbing , making it a worthy sport. Although it's a leisure sport, it also provides you a good exercise and helps you develop mentally and physically. It builds your endurance and mental acuity and challenges your endurance and perseverance.

In addition to helping improve your mental and physical well-being, but as an outdoor and indoor collaborative game, it gives you other advantages as well. When you're climbing outdoors, it a wonderful opportunity to take in the great outdoors as you soak in nature and breathe fresh air. It also provides an opportunity to make new acquaintances because it's an enjoyable social event. For instance, when you're climbing in indoor gyms, you'll see lots of people in the gym in a circle, cheering each other on, and even helping strangers. My experience has been welcomed by an incredibly large welcoming community since beginning my climb and it's been one of the most enjoyable things I've done. The overall experience of climbing is full of positive social and health advantages that make it a fantastic activity to take part in.

Intense Exercise

Rock climbing is definitely an extremely difficult sport. You're always working muscles aren't ones you normally perform in a normal workout for example, shoulders, back and elbows. Many say that after the initial climb it's typical that getting home difficult due to the intense work out on your arms. It's that hard. The sport demands the power of the whole body. Sometimes, the climber must tighten their muscles with great force when climbing. This helps to tone muscles, improves metabolism of your body, decreases fat and reduces calories and improves your stamina and endurance.

Stronger Arms

Climbing can aid in the building of stronger arms as a result of the constant usage of the walls. Particularly, on overhangs where rock faces are more that 90°, it is necessary to will need to exercise your arms hard to get to the top on the hill. After several weeks of consistently climbing, you'll notice that your strength and grip strength will improve.

Neck, back and shoulders

It also puts a powerful impact on the shoulders, which become more toned after a few weeks of hard work. The shoulders have to be able to stay in balance while you climbing. The neck and back muscles also get a active workout because it is your neck that has to gaze around for the next step in your journey.

Muscled Thighs

Your legs are always used to lift yourself off of the rocks. It is also common to make movements that require you to stretch your legs out a lot as well as position your legs in a strained position to stay balanced against the rock. Because of this pressure you'll build strong legs and the thighs.

Cardio

Climbing can be a intense exercise that increases heart rate, particularly when you're taking fewer breaks and are climbing fast. A study was published in which the energy expenditure along with the heart rate fourteen experienced climbers on an indoor wall was almost equal to the heart rate of those who run 8-11 minutes miles. Climbing is a full body aerobic workout that improves lung capacity and heart rate.

Mental and emotional benefits

Climbing does not only provide physical health benefits, but also offers psychological and mental benefits. It improves your intellectual capacity due to the problem-solving and strategy capabilities required for climbing. While climbing, you need to identify the route you'll take to achieve your goal, which demands you to work your brain. The more you are aware of the climbing techniques and the more you understand that it takes a lot of problem-solving to know the holds you must grasp, or the steps you have to do to overcome the difficulties. Because of this need for analytical thinking climbing improves your confidence in your strategic thinking when you are faced with many problems. It can also help relieve anxiety, increase your motivation and boost your confidence.

Relieves Stress

Climbing reduces stress levels. This may sound odd as on the one hand, you could be a little anxious when you're climbing a mountain struggling to find how to get to the summit without falling. The great thing about climbing isthat while taking part in the sport, it's all about climbing and staying focused at the moment. There is nothing else to think about while you're engaged in the sport. If you're worried over your daily struggles It's a great idea to climb because you'll likely take your mind off of all the stress and focus on how to get to the top of the mountain. It's a great way to distract yourself from your problems If you want to!

It boosts confidence

By achieving your goals for climbing and climbing regularly your confidence will rise. When you push yourself to the limit and face challenges repeatedly you'll start getting the belief that you're capable of whatever you want to do.

Develops Willpower

Climbing takes an enormous amount of determination because one is constantly determined to climb to the top. It requires a mindset of "I will not give up". Sometimes , when I climb, I feeling a boost of strength whenever I say to myself "I will not give up" and make myself push myself to the top. You'll be tempted to push yourself beyond your limits (as as long as it's safe) even when you're sure that you're likely to be thrown off. This kind of sport will help you persevere throughout life, as you'll always be challenged and will have to conquer hurdles.

I hope that the numerous rock climbing advantages will be enough to keep your interest in taking up the sport! As you can see, climbing rock can be beneficial to your health and it's always good to have a blast and be productive. If you're in search of an activity that helps build strength, tests your strategy, and improves your endurance, then you're at the right place.

Chapter 9: The Different Types Of Rock Climbing

After you've mastered the previous security tips, it's now the time to get familiar with the various types of rock climbing. There are a variety of rock climbing styles, and you'll have to determine which one is the most suitable one for you. Each style requires a specific set of equipment as well as specific locations and methods. For example, some individuals climb outdoors while others do it indoors. For indoor climbing helmets aren't typically required , but in outdoor climbing, it is essential to wear helmets when climbing the cliffs that are steep. There are climbers who use assistance with ropes and equipment to decrease the chance of falling, whereas others use ropes. This section will provide a variety of kinds of climbs are available to try.

The traditional climbing (known in the context of "trad climbing")

Trad climbing is frequently used in documentaries and films. Traditional climbing involves you climb up rock walls carrying your personal protective equipment, which includes steel, aluminum, brass chocks, nuts and slings, spring-loaded camming devices and tricams to stop your body in falling from. Trad climbing originates from ancient ways of climbing through walls using natural gear, by putting protective equipment onto walls, and then removing it while climbing. When you climb the wall, you place these nuts or cams in the rock's cracks using rope that is attached to the equipment to prevent you from falling back to the ground. This is known as placing gear and is the process of placing these gear pieces in the rock face, and then attaching the rope using a carabiner prior to climbing higher.

Trad climbing is founded on elements - like cracks or whatever you can find gear into - to secure your climb. Before the 1970's, climbers utilized pitons, which were hammered into the rock to assist in climbing. But, the pitons would be altered over time, which made them dangerous. With the advancement of technology, we are able to use spring-loaded devices for camming chocks, tricams and many more that are safer and safer within cracks. '

The installation of this equipment on rocks is an obstacle for the trad climbing. The equipment is costly and takes time to learn how to use it. Instead of climbing on pre-installed protection, you need to put this protective equipment yourself, which makes trad climbing an advanced form of climbing.

Trad climbing is more demanding as well as time-consuming and risky than other forms and is considered to be one of the most difficult types of climbing. As you can see, this style of climbing emphasizes self-sufficiency.

Sport Climbing

Sport climbing is like traditional climbing except that bolts remain fixed permanently in the cracks in the rock. In essence, the route is laid out and the climber only has to tie his gear onto each bolt in order to climb. While it's somewhat easier and safer than traditional climbing, it's nevertheless challenging. The distance of the climbing can be between 10 and 30 meters. it focuses a lot on endurance, flexibility, and strength. endurance.

Top Roping

In top rope climbing it's a rope connected onto an anchor a tight support on top of the rock or mountain and then hangs down to support the climber. It involves two individuals who climb on one side who's attached to the rope, as an belayer, who's on the ground and serves as an anchor or support on the climbing. Belayers wear a harness and an attached device to which the rope threads through. This way the belayer must be able to carry the total burden of the climber using only a little force. They are the primary source for the climber's security. In indoor rock gyms, belayers are usually required to undergo a short course to ensure they're capable of supporting climbers using appropriate methods. It is possible for something to be wrong, and the belayer should be well-trained since he is the primary person accountable for the climber using top rope.

Bouldering

Bouldering can be done without rope or other equipment. This kind of climbing is typically done on artificially constructed short structures, also known as rock walls. Personally, I like this kind of climbing the most because it requires the least amount of set up and has the lowest danger. Ropes aren't required because the highest height of rock wall or boulders is about 10 feet, which means the risk of injury is lower when a climber falls. To ensure safety, climbers should use chalk on their hands, to ensure they are dry and reduce the chance of falling. Bouldering mats can also be put at the base of the rock walls in order to protect against injuries by absorbing the impact if climbing. The use of bouldering mats and chalk are applicable to indoor and outdoor bouldering in bouldering gyms.

Free solo climbing

Free-single climbing is significantly more dangerous than the other forms of climbing mentioned previously. The climber climbs the walls on his own, without devices or ropes. If the climber falls, it could cause serious injury and even death. The person who climbs is completely dependent on his own abilities as well as physical strength, skill and confidence. If you're just starting out, I recommend that you not attempt this skill until you've mastered it!

Mountaineering

Mountaineering is a process of climbing by scrambling (a hike through a hill with your hands, and sometimes) as well as some easier climbs and crossing glaciers. The method of climbing has evolved into three distinct specializations such as snow craft, rock craft and skiing. Mountaineering can also be referred to as Alpinism within European languages because it involves climbing mountains that are as in the height of Alps. A few examples of locations for mountaineering are those in the Caucasus, Himalayas, Hindu Kush and more.

Crack Climbing

Crack climbing can be described as a kind of climbing where you must climb a crack on the wall employing a variety of techniques, including foot jams and hand jams (we'll discuss these in the future). Cracks can vary in terms of size. Sometimes the cracks are just sufficient that your fingers can fit inside , while some are wide enough that your whole body can be able to climb through it by stretching the legs.

Indoor Rock Climbing

Indoor rock climbing takes place on artificial structures, usually performed in an indoor climbing facility. Many people take it up to exercising (including me). Since outdoor climbing relies heavily on external factors like the right conditions for the environment indoor climbing has grown increasingly popular since it takes care of the issues and allows keen climbers and their exercise in. The main factors that limit outdoor climbing are weather and seasonal issues along with the increased chance of getting injured. With the help of supervisors, mats placed on floors, mats on the ground and pre-planned routes the indoor gyms for climbing are considered to be a little more secure.

It was the first climbing wall built using bricks, however today the structures are constructed by putting plywood on the frame of a metal. Spray coating is applied to these structures in order to create a appear more authentic. The indoor gyms usually allow you to perform toproping as well as bouldering and sport climbing.

For newbies I would recommend trying the top rope and bouldering at first. I would also advise to train in indoor gyms before taking on the outdoors. Most people discover that the transition between artificial rocks and real rock formations is a significant shift, as the latter is more challenging.

Chapter 10: Climbing Gear
Before climbing , you must check your safety equipment and climbing equipment. If you begin at an indoor gym these gyms typically will provide equipment rental. However, it's more beneficial to purchase your own equipment when you are looking to become more serious. The rental equipment will not be as good quality and well-fitting. Nine times out of 10 rental shoes won't be a perfect fit for your feet and having high-quality shoes will significantly enhance your performance. Rental equipment

will experience wear and tear over the course of time. Equipment must therefore be inspected prior to climbing and then purchased once you're ready and accelerate your climbing speed.

We'll now look at the equipment you need to buy. It is important to keep in mind that this isn't a comprehensive list of all the gear used in the various climbing methods, however, it does cover some of the essentials.

Rope and Webbing

Ropes are required in top roping, sports climbing and the trad climbing. There are two kinds of ropes that are used for climbing: low elongation ropes and dynamic ropes. These ropes are typically used for belaying and absorb the force from a fall. If you fall they will expand and the climber, the belayer and the equipment feel less pressure. Low-elongation ropes are able to stretch much less. Climbers generally utilize webbing that is composed from the combination of two kinds of ropes to have the best combination of the two. Webbing is a great choice to use as an anchor for the rocks or trees, or as a sort of harness to shield a rope or for carrying equipment.

Carabiners

Carabiners serve as connectors and are durable metal loops that have spring loaded openings that link climbers to their rope and safety equipment (like nuts, webbing, cams, bolts). In the past , they'd typically been made of steel, however now they are made mostly of aluminum alloy, which is lighter and more suitable to climb.

Harnesses

Climbers are wearing harnesses that hook on ropes. In indoor climbing gyms, you'll typically be provided with these harnesses for toproping. The loops on the between the two harnesses aid climbers tie on the rope using a figure-eight knot.

Different kinds of climbers utilize different harnesses. For instance sport climbers wear minimalist harnesses, while alpine climbers utilize light harnesses and large wall climbers utilize the padded harnesses. Sit harnesses are frequent when climbing rock. It has a belt for the waist, and two leg loops joined in at the top of your hips by an elastic loop known as belay loop. It gives plenty of space for movement while also ensuring a high level of security.

Quickdraws

Quickdraws consist of two carabiners with no locking that are joined to nylon/dyneema webbings. they connect rope to protective equipment. Quickdraws are typically used for climbing in indoor environments since they are already attached to walls. It is the safest way to attach the quickdraw while it's in waist height.

Belay Devices

Belay devices aid in controlling the rope while belayingand help protect climbers from falling. With a reliable device an infirm person can carry a heavier climber. They function by creating mechanical friction, which breaks falls when there is excess tension on the rope.

Protection Devices

Protective devices comprise nuts, hexes and spring loaded camming devices and tricams. These are tools that are installed as temporary supports on the rock in traditional climbs.

Climbing Helmet

Helmets keep your head safe from any debris that could fall from rock formations or cliffs. It is also a good idea to wear in the event of a fall that causes you to get your head hit. Helmets are mostly used for outdoor climbing, not indoor climbing. The majority of people don't wear helmets at indoor gyms since routes are already defined and there are also supervisors and mats with padding to ensure that people do not be injured.

Chalk

The use of chalk is by nearly all climbers to soak up sweat or moisture from their palms. The majority of climbers store chalk as a powder that is loose in a special chalk bag to ensure that there is no spillage. The bag is hung via an elastic strap from your harness to a belt that is worn around your waist so that you can replenish your chalk while climbing at a minimal effort.

Climbing Shoes

Climbing shoes have been specifically developed specifically for the sport, to enhance the gripping power of feet. If you were climbing at indoor gyms, you'd have to bring chalk and climbing shoes (or hire their rental). The soles of climbing shoes are constructed from rubber that has been vulcanized. The shoes themselves are just about a millimeter thick and sit very comfortably on the feet.

If you are looking to buy the right shoes for you, these are a few suggestions. The feet of your feet will swell throughout your day. Therefore, you should look for shoes to wear in the late afternoon. Do a workout or climb prior to shopping. If you are trying on shoes don't wear socks like you would normally be wearing socks while climbing. In terms of the right size, it is recommended to purchase shoes at least a size smaller than your usual shoes. Be flexible in your size since everyone's feet differ. The sole way to be certain that the fit is right for you is to test on these shoes at a store. I wouldn't recommend purchasing shoes on the internet. You can expect the fit to be painful slightly (but obviously not too much) while wearing them. Your feet may appear curled when wearing these shoes due to the tightness they are designed to fit.

Belay Gloves

Belay gloves are designed to safeguard the hands when laying the climber (you don't need gloves if you were the leader climber). These gloves are made of leather or synthetic materials that protects the hands from burns as well as accidental release from the rope.

Tape

Tape is used to protect your skin from cuts as well as fixing flappers (an accident caused by loose skin) as well as preventing tendon injuries by binding the wrists and fingers.

Haul Bag

An haul bag an enormous robust bag in which climbing equipment can be put into.

If this all seems intimidating, don't be concerned. Continue reading the next section and figure out the essential equipment requirements as you move along. If you are starting climbing indoors, you can start with rental equipment initially.

To make sure you grasp all the equipment needed to climb I suggest you visit the local store for sportswear for outdoor activities. You can browse through all the gear listed on this page. Take a look at the various types of equipment needed. For a start I'd recommend looking into the way climbing shoes fit you. If you decide to start climbing indoors in gyms, it is possible to check the way that new shoes feel as opposed to the way the rental ones feel.

Chapter 11: Safety Tips

Climbing can be exciting and thrilling but it is also a risk. Beginners are more prone to accidents because they may not be aware of proper methods of climbing and safety precautions. Always take care to avoid injury and take lessons with a qualified instructor prior to beginning.

Warm-Up and Stretch

Stretching and warming up before climbing can reduce muscle stiffness and improve flexibility. It improves blood circulation to muscles, which facilitates the ease of contraction and relaxation to improve muscle elasticity. It is recommended to do stretching exercises that stretch the shoulders arms and forearms hips and waists and knees, as well as feet and ankles prior to going up.

Check Your Harness

The safety of climbers depends on the appropriate usage and the condition of their harness. The average lifespan of a harness is about 10 years since it is degraded when exposed to moisture, sunlight or other environmental factors. When you first begin climbing, it is recommended to conduct an inspection of the harness, and inspect the webbing, the tie-in points, as well as the loop that holds your belay for tear and wear. The buckles must be double-back and the harness should never be placed in contact with acidic solutions, caustic solutions or light sources that are excessive. It is recommended to wash it by hand with the water of lukewarm and kept in a cool, dark location.

Wear a Helmet

Helmets worn during climbing outdoors is essential during climbing and belaying because it could be life-threatening if the head isn't protected. Helmets protect your head from rocks falling on it or injuries from falling.

Verify the Rope and the Belay device.

For a safe climb , it is essential that the rope and belay device are in good state of repair. It is important to ensure that the rope is connected to the devices for the belay. This implies that the rope and the belay device are secured with a lock carabiner to the belay loop of the harness of the belayer.

Use Anchors that are safe

The climber must always utilize at minimum two anchors near high points on the pitch or along the route. Three anchors are the best. For sport climbing, one must make use of locks on carabiners.

Correctly clip the Rope

Check that you've correctly clipped the rope to the carabiner. Don't back-clip. Back-clipping occurs when you are leading an upward climb, but you do not properly attach the rope to the carabiner at the bottom. The rope is released from the carabiner towards the rock. This is difficult because there's possibility that the rope could unclip itself. Make sure the rope is exiting the carabiner away from the rock.

Climb using the Rope over your leg

It is always better to place the rope on the legs, rather than in between or beneath them. The rope should be kept between the legs, and in front of them could cause the climber to fall down upside down if stumbles and slips, which can result in the climber hitting his head.

Pay Attention!

It's impossible to predict what might occur while climbing. Climbers should pay attention and ensure that they don't be distracted. For instance, if you're in the process of laying another climber, be attentive to the climber in front of you. He's the one who's at risk of being injured and falling Don't use your mobile phone or speak to others climbing while you're being laid. If you're climbing walls, you must be aware of falling rocks and unstable holds.

Plan Every Step

Climbers should look for rocks and sketch out their routes prior to climbing. Before taking any step, you should be able to see clearly in your head of the direction each hold will take. In order to do this, you must acquire sufficient knowledge of the various methods of climbing, which differ depending on the rock you are climbing. An understanding of all this will aid in avoiding injuries. We'll discuss climbing techniques in the next sections.

Always Learn

It is essential to continue learning through your errors, analyzing other climbers and their methods and also reading materials. Simply watching other climbers as well as reading books on climbing (like these) can help tremendously, since they will give you good advice on the most common mistakes.

Bring the Correct Gear and Bring Enough Gear

The climber must always have sufficient safety equipment prior to climbing. Use an extended climbing rope that is able to easily reach the anchor and then lower to the ground without difficulty. Bring a few bolts and nuts, and ensure that you are wearing your helmet as well as climbing shoes and other equipment previously mentioned. In addition you must also carry water bottles and snacks when you go out in the open to keep well-hydrated and healthy.

Do not climb alone

Climbers who are new to climbing should not be climbing alone. Although free solo climbing is climbing on your own it is advised to do the sport with friends watching the climber. If you're just beginning your climb should not begin by climbing solo because it can be very risky. Climbers must take an experienced climber or a leader who can offer guidance on how to lower the risk.

Be aware of your limits

When you're outdoors climbing it's vital to be aware of your limits. Sometimes, I'll push my limits while climbing indoors, however, climbing gyms are safer because they offer pre-planned paths and mats for climbing. To stay safe, especially outdoors, climbers should not try to make moves that they won't be able to make.

Now you know how to start climbing, from understanding the various types of climbing to getting started with the equipment and safety. It is possible to begin climbing on rocks, but the next segments will assist you to understand the basics that will enhance your climbing skills.

Chapter 12: The Different Types Of Faces

Once you've got a good grasp of safety protocols as well as the equipment you'll need, it's now time to get to know more about rocks themselves. Faces are among the many kinds of rock formations you'll come across. In essence, you'll see three types of rocks: slabs horizontal faces and overhangs.

Slabs

Slabs are rocks that are not more that 90° in angles. They're more smooth than vertical faces and overhangs. When climbing on slabs, one has to know how to make use of his feet while maintaining an ideal balance. It is recommended to wear slippery climbing shoes to improve the friction between your feet and rock. To climb a slab you must keep the majority the weight of you on your feet. The arms and hands are utilized for balance, instead of pulling while your feet are utilized for moving forward. Some of the most popular areas for climbing slabs include Tuolumne Meadows in California, South Platte Area in Colorado as well as Looking Glass Mountain in North Carolina.

To climb slab routes , you must read the rocks for weak points and features that you could utilize as holds, since there aren't so many holds for these kinds of rocks. When climbing slabs, you have to be calm and composed to remain in control.

Smearing is the principal technique employed to climb slabs. The feet are directly placed on the surface of the rock as it is not equipped with any holding devices or features. The climber applies pressure as well as the friction created between their shoes and rock aids the climber in climb higher. A good smearing technique results in greater surface contact and less friction between rock and shoe. The shoe should be kept flat , not with a pointed tip to allow for better smears.

The performance of a slab climb is largely contingent on the shoes of the climber techniques, the type of rock, and the the type of rock. For instance, rocks with 60 degrees angle are more difficult to smear compared to those closer to 90 degrees. Granite or sandstone rocks that have more jagged edges are less difficult to climb than smooth quartzite rocks.

It is essential that climbers keep their center of gravity higher than the ground when on a slab. If you are too in close proximity to the wall can lead to the possibility of your feet sliding off the wall. To ensure that they stay upright the climber must utilize their hands in order to position himself with a small amount of a distance between his hip and the rock.

A slab climb needs gentle movements, not unnatural movements. The climber shouldn't employ dynamic techniques in this circumstance (dynamic moves require strength and speed). To keep their equilibrium, climbers should perform a few steps. If the climber slips and falls, the climber should attempt to stand up instead of falling, to prevent severe skin injury.

Vertical Faces

The vertical rock face is the most typical in the types of rock you expect from a typical climb. They are inclined about 90 ° and almost vertical. When climbs on vertical rock face, the foot is crucial. It is essential to keep your weight on your feet for as long as you can. The techniques for footwork include inside edge, outside edging and spreading. Alongside footwork it is also necessary to locate where your centre of gravity is, and utilize your hands and arms to pull on the holds. Some of the top vertical climbs are Shelf Road within Colorado, Smith

Rock in Oregon, New River Gorge in West Virginia, and Shawngunks in New York.

Overhang Faces

Faces that are angled over 90 degrees are called overhanging faces. Overhangs have a slope that is higher than vertical and require lots in upper-body strength. The top climbing overhangs located in America are The Rifle Mountain Park in Colorado, American Fork in Utah as well as The Red River Gorge in Kentucky. Overhangs that appear to be vertical and hence more powerful are referred to as roofs.

It is hard to climb overhangs. and exhausting. Make sure your arms are in a straight line and relax your muscles keep your muscles relaxed, and pull just when you have to pull to conserve energy. Because of the steepness the arms are utilized more often than legs, and there are fewer rest places than the vertical faces of rock. In this case, the climber has to keep their center of gravity as close as possible to the rock in order to maintain an intense body tension. Techniques for footwork include hooks for the heel and toe for putting less pressure on the arms.

Tips and Tricks

It's not just about strength. It requires a great deal of planning to conserve energy, improve efficiency, and attain holds that are more challenging for people of average height. If you are able to master the right knowledge and regular practice, climbers will rapidly improve their skills. Through learning the basic principles, you can effectively maintain balance, movement and endurance needed to climb.

Do your best to climb with your legs

A lot of novice climbers focus only on their arms when they climb but it's also easy to overlook the fact you're legs equally important to your arms. The arms are meant to be used to balance points and your legs should be used as pistons that push you forward. If you're stuck, look to the side instead of upwards to check if your legs could assist you. When you're climbing be sure to look for higher footholds to ensure you are supported and stable.

Regarding footholds, be sure to make sure you're taking smaller steps rather than larger ones since it requires more strength to get up from holds which are further from each other. Shoes for climbing can help in your legs to work because they possess more sticky substances inside their soles. The small protrusions of the walls can make great for footholds, as long as you're confident in them and put them under pressure when standing. Make sure you trust your hold - you can lose lots of energy and energy when you're constantly checking around and not trusting the grips you're using.

It is easy to spot the beginning climber when you see climbers gripping handholds with both hands, and then attempt to climb with their feet hanging. This is a waste of energy and makes it difficult to climb to the top if you're not able to do it. Make sure you have at least three limbs in your wall all time (2 hands one foot, or one hand and two feet).

Acceleration of Climbing

Two ways to categorize the speed and means by the can climb: static motion and dynamic motion.

Static motion is fluid and slow. With static motions you'll be in control and constantly moving as your body is balanced. While performing this type of climb your feet will remain in the wall for the entire duration. You'll be capable of pull your body upwards to a certain position and then take the next step without creating energy or turning. Thus, each limb is moved will be weightless carefully, and manipulated with great control and preciseness.

For static movements, attempt to control your movements and stay clear of unneeded actions. To achieve this, you must learn how to only contract the essential muscles (usually the shoulders, forearms abs, thighs, as well as calves) and be conscious of any tension in muscles that use up more energy (muscles that are located in the upper arm and legs, hips as well as the neck, torso and the face). Repositioning and moving around can cause you to fall or lose your balance.

Dynamic motion demands power and momentum. When you perform dynamic movements you're basically moving from balance into imbalance, then back to equilibrium. Dynamic moves are utilized when you need to shift your center of gravity beyond your comfort zone, and reach higher than you typically would. For dynamic movements that move your body more quickly, you must move it with greater power, and maybe avoid holding. Your feet will also be able to move off the walls and then put them back in whenever you're required to. Moving with speed allows you to gain more ground by each step, however, you'll use more force and energy.

Plan Your Route

It's important to know your routes. The planned routes will aid in improving your climbing since you'll be aware of the moves you'll need make as you go. Before you begin climbing, imagine the sequences you'll need to complete the route, taking into consideration your weight and balance and range of each move. Sometimes it is helpful to imagine yourself at the top of the climb, and then go backwards along the route taking notes of the movements of your feet and hands. in relation to the place you are.

Once you've completed the route, get back at ground level and take a review the route. It is a good habit to map your routes and then re-evaluate routes. The more you practice, the more proficient you'll be.

Find resting spots

While you may be able to reach your goal quicker with speed climbing, it's helpful to make rest breaks in the right spots along your journey. Make use of these places during your climb, so that you'll get back your energy. Climbers who seek out and utilize rest places will perform much better than people who do not since endurance is a major factor. To achieve this, try reclining some by leaning back against the edge of the wall or keeping your knee beneath an overhang. For every 3 metres of climb, climbers should take a break and rest.

Gain Reach

Reach backwards when climbing as a beginner, the majority of climbers want to be facing the next climb because they're planning to reach the hold. However, shifting their gaze off from the hold, and moving backwards could allow more reach than the forward one, due to the shape of our shoulders.

Stand Up - Newbies often not use their legs when climbing. If you're bent on your knee on a stand, you must stand up with your legs to maximize the benefit that the holds offer. This increases the extension that you have every foot hold, making it's easy to reach every handhold. Also, with every hand hold you need to be sure to straighten your arms so that you don't strain your biceps. If you keep your hips parallel to the floor, that will assist to straighten your legs naturally.

Bumping

Bumping is an excellent method to get up to an effective hold. There are times when you'll be in an position that allows you to get a hold that is small but it's difficult to keep the hold. There may be an additional hold which is more appealing. In this scenario it's possible to make a bump by getting to the lower hold, and then quickly getting off it, and then use it to increase your speed in order to reach the higher-quality hold.

Chapter 13: Handholds And Grips

Handholds for rock climbing work similar to the bars on an incline or railings of the staircase. To climb higher, you must be holding the holds with hands to ensure equilibrium. There are a variety of handholds with different dimensions, shapes and texture. Grips and holds define the sequence of your movements while climbing.

Although the alignment of the feet and body is crucial to climbing however, mastering the gripping holds is equally crucial. To define the qualities of a handhold, we make use of the term "positivity" that refers to the ease at that a person maintains contact with the grip. The positivity of a grip is related to how much force is needed to stick i.e. the higher the positive is, the lower the energy or force needed.

To master how to grasp various handholds, it is important to have to begin doing it by practicing at an indoor climbing center. The indoor climbing trails include a variety of handholds made by humans that will help you master each kind of grip. It also aids in building the strength of your hand and forearms. In essence, the three primary methods to grip handholds are 1. Pull down, 2. Pull in the opposite direction, and then 3. Pull upwards.

Edges

The most commonly used kinds of handholds that climbers will encounter are the edges and flat surfaces that are 90 degrees in a 90-degree angle to the walls. Edges are typically horizontal flat holds with a positive exterior however, they can be rounded as well. Certain edges are equipped with lips to allow climbers to pull out from the edge. They're either large or thin and range from 1.5 inches and 18 inches wide. The longer edges are known as buckets or Jugs.

To grip edges with a firm grasp You can use two strategies using the full crimp grasp or the wide hand grip or half crimp grip. When you grip with a crimp, you grasp the edge with your fingers, flatly on top , and your fingers positioned above the tips. The fingers' pads are laid on the edge, as well as the fingers curled to ensure it is that your second joint gets bent sharply. The thumb is then placed over the index finger to secure it. Locking the thumb will make the grip stronger.

The grips are usually made on limestone and granite cliffs. However, with this technique there's a chance of injury to joints and tendons of your fingers in the event that you're not crimping enough. In the event that you are constantly clamping you're at risk of developing a chronic injury that will not heal. It is therefore recommended not to use this kind of grip when you have other handholds available.

However open hand grips often referred to as half-crimp grips, are excellent for sloping edges. They are typically used for narrow edges where the pads of the fingers can be conveniently put. It is best to use them when there's a lots of friction between the skin and rock. This way it's not necessary to have the full crimp grip, and your fingers will be grateful. If you can, opt for the half-crimp grip instead or the full-crimp one to decrease the likelihood of permanent damage to fingers and tendons. You can work on your half crimp in indoor climbing gyms and while climbing to increase your crimp's strength, so it isn't too much of it, and you're at risk of damaging.

Pins

Pinches are a distinct type of handhold. They have two opposing sides and can be used to grip. They are generally held by the whole hand, however any grip that utilizes the thumb against the other hand to increase the positive impact of the grip is regarded as an a pinch.

They can appear like two edges emerging out of the rock , shaped like a book , or appear as tiny knobs. In smaller pinches the thumb is in opposition to your index finger or towards both index finger and middle finger. They are stacked on top of one another (which is the most effective alternative). The larger pinches are usually more manageable to hold.

Slopers

Slopers are handholds that have a rounded shape , and don't have distinct edges or lips that are designed to grasp. They typically are found on slab climbs which are rocks which are not as angled, making them easy for novices. Slab climbs are angled about 45-75 degrees, while typical climbs have 90 degrees of angular.

Slopers also require an open hand grip/half crimp grasp and rely on an abrasion of skin to the rock's surface. Slopers are the most beneficial when they are placed above the climber and not in the direction that the climber. This is because the climber is able to straighten his arms when the slopers are in front of the climber. This gives the climber the maximum leverage. Cool , dry weather, instead of hot and humid conditions makes slopers more comfortable to utilize.

For the best grip from a sloper utilize your hands to look for a bump or ridge. Most often, you'll find a part that is easy to hold and you can utilize fingers to rub the sloper using your fingers together, then apply pressure to it.

Pockets

Pockets are shallow or deep pockets that climbers hold onto with the use of four fingers. Pockets are different in size, from oval to oblong in shape and be also different in depth. They're mostly located within limestone rocks.

Pockets that are big enough to hold with one hand are referred to as monodoigt pockets. For smaller pockets, make use of your most powerful fingers. For 1-finger pockets, you need to use your middle finger and for pockets that have two fingers, make use of your middle and index fingers.

If using pockets as handholds climbers should make use of the most fingers possible due to the bigger surface area that can be used for friction. In the pocket, climbers must look for dimples that could be utilized to pull against. Once you've located the best portion of the pocket to hold on it, you can pull down on it to gain leverage. Pockets on rocks that slope are actually used to serve as an alternative side pull and it is possible to pull along the sides rather than the bottom, to remove them. Because this type handhold requires the fingers frequently it is more likely of injury to the tendons therefore, make sure you don't over-practice your hands.

Sidepulls

Sidepulls, also known as layaways are edges that are placed either vertically or diagonally, and are placed to your side, rather than over you. They're utilized to pull away from instead of downwards. they work because you're fighting the pulling force using your feet or with another hands. For instance, you'd lean to the right when the sidepull was on your left, as an equalization against opposing forces. Sidepulls also work well when you tilt your hip toward the wall and sit at the outer edge of your climbing shoe. This allows the other hand to reach high.

Gastons

The name was given to the gaston in honor of Gaston Rebufatt who was a elegant French climber. Gastons are like sidepulls in that they are horizontal or diagonal angles. They are typically used in the front of your face or your torso. To ensure a solid grip on the handhold, hold it in your hands by placing your palms in front of the rock with your thumb facing downwards. It is bent to an acute angle and is pointing away from your body. Similar to the side pull gastons, they require a fight by your feet. They can be found on many routes and make good hands to practice with.

Undercling

Underclings are handholds gripped on the underside of its surface with fingers clinging to its edge on the outside. They are available in a variety of designs, like cracks that are horizontal or diagonal and pockets. They can also be inverted edges, inverted edges and flakes.

To hold these holds You hold the undercling with your four fingers into the crack, then face your palm upwards, and then point your thumb to the outside. You can then climb by pulling your fingers away from the undercling and putting your feet on the wall. This kind of handhold works best when the handhold is located near your mid-section. Use straight arms to lessen fatigue since these hold are strenuous.

Palming

If there is no handhold found on the outdoor wall You can try hand-holding the wall. It is done by pressing your fingers on the rock and relying on the friction between your hands and rocks to pull off from. The palm's heel helps keep your hands in place on the rock, and lets you push away from it. Palming is typically used for slab climbs with no handholds that are specifically designed for it. It also helps conserve energy since you're pushing instead of pulling.

For a palming handhold look for a small crease on the surface of the rock and then use your palm to put it on the rock. Push downwards on the stone using the palm of your hand. This will let you move your foot to a foothold, with your weight centered the palm of your hands.

You can also play around with dihedrals or the inside corners of walls that are vertical. Dihedrals are the places where two wall surfaces meet. To imagine the situation Imagine a book that is open lying on a table. Then imagine yourself trying to climb it by pushing the covers off. When climbing these dihedrals the palming technique involves pushing your fingers against walls and pushing them up.

Hands Matching

Matching hands is a method that is used by climbers to match their hands with each other on a handhold that is large that is usually a wide border or rail on the rock. This technique assists in switching hands to ensure that the next hold is easily reached. Hands that match are more appropriate when holding large-sized holds because there is more room to put both hands. It is much more difficult to do this with smaller holds. If you have to try this with a smaller hold, try using a couple of fingers to grip the holds instead of using your entire hand. Once you've got your match your second hand swiftly move your first hand from the grip and into the following.

Hand Jamming

Hand jamming is one the most effective climbing techniques for crack climbs. This method involves inserting your hands in the cracks in the rock with your thumbs upwards. By tucking the thumb inside the palms the palms of both hands extend your hand until there is a contrasting pressure on the rocks between the hands. In essence, your hand will be trapped in a crack. it is secured, you are able to put your weight on the wall.

To ascend with this movement, continue to move your hands along the crack. Moving your upper hand upwards and then follow it with the lower hand to continue the motion to go upwards. There are often tiny holds in cracks you can discover to help you move forward. Hand jamming is usually followed with foot jams. These will be discussed in the section on foot techniques.

Mantle (Technique that requires mainly Triceps)

Although it's not a form of grip, or handhold it is a movement that relies on arms to help climb up to an unobstructed horizontal surface of an obstruction. I've included this technique in this category because it's a method that mostly requires strength in the triceps and specific hand movements (and additionally, some footwork in order to raise yourself from the floor).

Mantling is akin as when you're trying to escape from an in-ground pool without an ladder. In this scenario, the climber needs to hold his hands close to the edge to keep his balance, and then move forward. Instead of pulling the way you would normally do when climbing, press and push to rise. Following that, the climber needs to raise his foot to the ledge or on another holding device. Stretching before the climb can help immensely when it comes to this.

Chapter 14: Footwork Techniques

The use of footwork can aid greatly in improving your climbing skills. There are many footwork methods we'll discuss and the implementation of at the very least two or three of these techniques can make a huge difference in climbing effectively for novices. Footwork methods reduce strain on the forearms, and can help the body to reach higher holds with ease. In addition, leg muscles have more endurance and energy than arms, which contributes to greater friction force and more powerful gripping.

Moving Your Legs Up by Pushing

Like I said before that pushing up using your legs to reach a higher ascent is vital. Many beginners do not realize the importance of using their legs. Standing on a foot stand you can increase the reach of your arms.

Be active and watch your feet

The most experienced climbers will examine their footholds and feet prior to reaching up using their arms. Be aware to your foot and make sure you move it ahead of your hands as often as you can.

Training on footholds

You can practice the movements of your feet and exercises. Utilize two handholds using your hands and put your feet on the edges. Do two steps, one for each foot, and then move to an upper handhold. Once you've got this down the habit of paying attention to footholds will come more easily.

Learn to work with various kinds of footholds

After you've mastered these basic skills and you're paying close attention at your feet it's time to work on more advanced techniques. There will be occasions that your feet will need to test smaller, more challenging footholds, or with different types of designs. Test out which footholds are the most effective and what weight your feet are able to support with smaller grips. Begin to trust your feet. We'll go over some techniques that are used for these holds that are irregular and methods later.

Smearing

Smearing can be very helpful when climbing slabs that are not held, but have there is a greater diagonal slope (less the vertical slope). This method is based on putting pressure on the blank portion of the rock using the assistance of the bottoms of the toes. This way you're trying to improve your contact with the rocks and sole of your shoes to ensure that there is enough friction to remain in the rocks. To make it be effective, it's recommended that you're using the smearing technique using rocks that are not as vertical as described earlier.

You'll be amazed at how walls of rock that appear empty aren't really empty and can actually create enough friction if you believe in that. You'll be amazed at how the rubber inside your shoes actually is more sticky than you believe. If you're able to trust it and put your foot over the tiny crystals, then you'll stand on these bare surfaces.

Foot Jamming

Foot jamming is a great technique for cracks that can be handled. When using foot jamming the climber must lift his feet up to the level of his shins, then lower his knees to the side of the crack and keep the soles of his footwear parallel to the crack. The toe is to be inserted to the side of the crack and then cammed into place. With this method but there is the possibility of being stuck with your foot in cracks. To avoid this, do not over-wedge. Also, leave a little bent when standing up to allow you to lower the knee when you need to free your foot from the jammed foot.

Crossovers

Crossovers are a fantastic technique for those who want to walk sideways over walls. To accomplish this, extend your hand to your side to secure it and then cross one leg over the other in order to grab for a foothold. This will allow you to shift your weight and shift from in a side-to-side manner.

Backstepping

Backstepping is an excellent method to utilize in overhangs. Overhangs are the rocks which are at more than 90 degrees. Therefore, you need to be able to hang beneath the rock while keeping your back nearly as close to the ground.

When you backstep, you turn the hips (and leg) to ensure that your outside hips face the rock. This opens your torso, so that you are able to reach greater lengths by using the other foot, in the direction that you've reversed.

Flagging

By flagging, you're using your legs as a support instead they're being used to balance the weight mechanism. When you flag, just need to point one limb (usually the leg) to make sure you don't swing too far away from the rock. It is possible to swing the limb in front towards you, or in the back of according to your preferred route. If you choose to flag behind your hips, they remain in a straight line and your active leg doesn't exert much pressure, so it's a more challenging alternative. Be aware that when you employ this method, you're not touching the rock even if you're hitting the wall's wall using the leg you're flagging.

Stemming

Stemming is a great technique for footwork that doesn't require excessive energy when you're pushing against walls using your legs, and applying opposing forces. This technique is most effective on dipherals. Apply force in opposite directions to your legs so you can move smooth and easily with minimal effort. These forces cause enough friction to allow your hands to move when done properly, you'll be able to rest on your hands. Imagine climbing the chimney using your legs. It's what it's like. It requires the right balance, technique and flexibility for stemming , but once you've mastered it, it's a great feeling and looks nice!

Heel Hooking

Heel hooking is an advanced form of footwork, which demands the climber put the foot's heel onto a rung typically at waist level or greater. It's an innovative method that requires keeping the body in close proximity to the wall and keeping the arms in a flexible position, letting you climb up walls or even out of the roof. Hooking the heel is a fantastic technique for climbing aretes (a edge that is cleaved where wall and ceiling connect) as well as on the ledges. It can help you maintain the balance in more difficult climbs, where the rocks can be angled in a way and you have to think up a new strategy to tackle your climb.

The most important aspect of making a heel hook is how much pressure that you apply to your leg to hold the heel hook in position. It is also necessary to engage the muscles of the hamstrings. Alongside helping with stability, heel hooking assists in removing weight from hands and arms. This lets you have breaks between. For a proper execution of the heel hooks correctly, it's recommended to wear climbing shoes and regularly increase your strength and flexibility.

Toe Hooks

Toe hooks, just like the name, work with your toes, not your heel. Instead of pressing against your heel, you should pull off your toes. The pressure is essential in this technique. Toe hooks are utilized on the same rock as heel hooks they are excellent to keep your body in place while avoiding swinging, as well as to rest.

The ability to master these foot movements can help you move more quickly in your progression. Most beginners don't utilize their legs, so make use of your legs to stay balanced and extend your the reach of your feet.

Chapter 15: What Makes Climbing Mountains Dangerous And Difficult?

I'm not the type of person to let people down when I set out plans but I didn't want to climb an mountain as I woke up around 5.30 am. I was willing to say yes, however, and I set to meet my students and teachers. We were traveling into Slovenia going up into the hills until I got to the parking area, and I looked around and wondered how you can climb up the parking lot because it was so steep. I've been told we'll zig-zag up and down which is why it takes the time. The ascent began at 7.30 am. I was wearing the Doctor Marten boots since my hiking boots were not in England and I began to realize the magnitude of the challenge ahead just a few minutes. We quickly climbed, which means that oxygen levels fell quickly and I realized that it was becoming difficult to breathe. Because I couldn't breathe physical I had to keep stopping which made me anxious.

After a while I realized that it wasn't going be easy it was just mud and rocks! This has become exhausting! It took us 5 hours to get to the top. I thought we wouldn't be able to get there, but the moment we made it I was awestruck. The views were breathtaking as we were high above the clouds and surrounded by hills. The view was stunning. We were able to see Austria, Slovenia and Italy. It was amazing and I was satisfied that I could do it. Then I received the negative news through one of my classmates. He said that the downhill was more difficult. I was ready to quit, but we were stuck with no way to get out.

We began our descent. It was more comfortable to breathe, however it was much more difficult to breathe underfoot. We walked down an alternative path that was longer. I was still sliding and became exhausted. The other people with me (who have a habit of climbing mountains) were in agreement that it was a gruelling and difficult work. My entire body was aching. When I could feel the weight of every stone, I was constantly falling over while my ankles were in a throbbing. I started to cry while we sat down to take an rest. What I was unable to comprehend was how we'd be able to return, after 8 hours of walking, and then drinking water that was drained. I found the strength and was able to walk down. We were welcomed by the other participants who were clapping. It was 6.30 pmand eleven hours had passed.

2.1 What are the hazards of mountain climbing?

Climbing mountains is a risky sport. If the mountain is regarded as "safe" and frequented by old and young tourists the chance of injuries will never be minimal.

What are the risks of climbing mountain peaks? The biggest risk in climbing mountains is the lack of information. There are risks to the environment associated with rock climbing. Sometimes, it's the risks created by human activity which can cause fatal consequences.

It doesn't mean that you'll never be able to climb a rock. In light of the previous accidents that occurred beware of those mountainous areas What should you do is be aware of and be prepared for risks that might be present.

What is Mountain Climbing Dangers: Possible Risques?

Mountain climbing is a dangerous sport. When the mountain is regarded as "safe" and frequented by both old and young travelers the danger of accidents is never small.

What are the dangers of climbing mountain peaks? The most significant risk associated with climbers is deficiency of understanding. There are environmental dangers that could be a result associated with rock climbing.

Sometimes, it's the risks created by human activity which can cause tragic outcomes.

However, this doesn't mean you'll never be able to climb a rock. In light of the previous accidents that have occurred Avoid those mountain peaks What should you do is to be aware and be prepared for potential dangers that could be lurking.

Be aware of your deficiency of awareness.

Let's discuss the lack of understanding before we dive in the dangerous world of climbing mountains.

* Overconfidence could be due to a lack of knowledge. A small amount of knowledge can be more damaging than having no knowledge. It is possible to think that you are an expert but do not listen to the advice of those who might be smarter than you.

Lack of knowledge could also be due to an absence of knowledge or information if you do not understand what risk is and you don't be able to know how or where to remain in a safe place.

* How do you get your attention to work?

- Say to yourself that you don't have anything to do (much).

As a climber, be aware that seeking assistance and direction is essential to your achievement.

* Join with others who have more experience. Just by watching them, you will learn a lot.

Begin by tackling smaller and easier climbs and observe the issues you're facing. Have a buddy with you!

* Do what is told to you. If a sign tells you to remain out, stay out. Take note of any person who advises you against this, it's not the best idea.

* You should not perform something you're not fully aware of. Perhaps you'll gain knowledge from your experience. However, you don't have another chance.

* Err, I'm on the right track. I'd rather be secure rather than brave in climbing on rocks.

1. Altitudes Elevated Altitudes

Low altitudes can cause the onset of sickness at high altitudes. According to the official Death Zone has elevations greater than 26,000 feet (8,000 meters). There is also the risk of permanent brain damage, even if there is no altitude-related sickness while hiking.

At altitudes that are high low oxygen levels result in a decrease of oxygen levels in the body. This leads to vomiting when you are at an altitude.

* The symptoms of altitude sickness are likely to develop at elevations of 8000 feet (2,500 meters).

* The long oxygen deprivation cycle destroys brain cells as well as other cells. This causes brain damage over the long-term.

* The degree of sickness at altitude can vary in severity from mild to severe. In different people, it can occur at different altitudes.

Mild sickness at altitude (also called Acute Mountain Sickness (AMS)):

* Headache, difficulty sleeping nausea, dizziness exhaustion, shortness in breath, a lack of appetite, sleep issues and general lack of energy are all signs.

Symptoms typically begin at an altitude that is high within 12 to 24 hours after the time of landing.

* After an hour or so mild altitude sickness will go away after rest as you adjust to the elevation. It is essential that prior to climbing, you take the time to adjust and access your body's needs.

* Learn how to improve your sleeping at higher altitudes when walking.

* The symptoms are more severe and cannot be cured by prescription medications.

Instead of improving over time, symptoms such nausea, fatigue and shortness of breath get worse.

*Confusion, inability to balance, difficulty walking and a worsening headache not cured by medications and vomiting, fatigue or chest tightness all signs. It's difficult to perform normal tasks, but you'll still be capable of walking by yourself (might be a bit shaky).

* Symptoms include a shortness of breathing during rest and coughing. Other symptoms include noisy breathing (gurgling or the sound of rattling) and fever (maybe with a frothy spewing). This is a pulmonary embolism manifestation at high altitude (HAPE) that is, when there is a risk of a buildup of fluids within the lung.

* Tiredness, extreme confusion and trouble walking. It can cause severe nausea, headache, and general fatigue. This is a sign of cerebral edema in high-altitude (HACE) that occurs when the brain is able to store blood.

* Lip color, skin color and fingernails: gray light or blueish.

How do you keep altitude sickness from happening and prevent injury in the brain?

• Acclimatize prior to ascending to higher altitudes.

* Stay short, remain in the low (er). Recent studies have revealed that brain injury could occur at an elevation as high as 16000 feet (4,800 meters)

If you are suffering from the symptoms of altitude sickness. What should you do?

* To help with the process of acclimatization, it is important to rest and sleep to avoid the mild symptoms of altitude sickness.

* Consider taking medications that could help with symptoms, like Acetazolamide (Diamox) or Dexamethasone. Before you take any medication or medication at altitudes above

2,000 feet it is crucial to follow the advice of your doctor.

* Return to a lower altitude. A life-threatening condition is extreme altitude sickness that can turn deadly in just a few hours. You should quickly lower to a lower elevation.

2. Extreme Temperatures

There is a risk of getting heat-related wounds while climbing in a hot climate. Heat stroke and exhaustion are the most common causes of heat stroke.

The body may lose heat too rapidly when you climb in cold conditions. This could lead to frostbites as well as hypothermia.

Exhaustion caused by the heat

* This is caused by the body's overheating.

The symptoms include heavy sweating, dizziness fainting, weak and rapid heartbeat headache, nausea, fatigue are all signs.

* What's needed to be done:

* Sit in shade, drink ice cold drinks or water.

* If the condition persists you should consult a physician.

In the heat, a heart attack:

You may get heatstroke if you suffer from heat exhaustion and are not addressed.

* Fever (temperature over 100 F (40 C)) Dry skin, dizziness the pounding of your heart, headache fatigue, nausea, anxiety, and loss of consciousness are signs.

What's next:

* Relax in the shade, drink ice cold water or a sports drink.

Use water, spongesor ice packs/wet towels to cool your body. Get rid of any excess clothing.

* Immediately seek medical attention.

Hypothermia AKA Hypothermia

* This is caused by the loss of body heat.

* Temperatures dropping lower than 95 F (35 C), chills, slow and shallow breathing, weak heartbeat blurred vision, fatigue, the loss of consciousness are all signs.

What's next:

Take off all cold or damp clothes Cover with dry, warm blankets and clothing, and move to an air-conditioned and dry spot.

* Drink hot or warm drinks.

For medical attention.

3. Natural disasters

An natural disaster, unfortunately isn't something you need to be prepared for. Maybe, at any time an earthquake or volcano eruption could occur.

These accidents may be rare however, the results are usually serious.

Here are some possible natural disasters you might confront during a climb:

* Typhoons/storms

* Earthquake Over

* Volcano eruptions

* Avalanche Avalanche

What can cause you to be trapped by an natural disaster:

* In off-season when the mountains are ascending. In most cases, due to the greater chance of natural hazards, mountains can be locked.

* It's just luck occasionally.

What happens during an natural disaster if you are in the middle?

Severe wounds or death.

* Getting lost. Access could be blocked and the routes could be blocked or impaired. It may be difficult to locate the exit and it may be a long time before you reach you for assistance.

* How to avoid getting caught up during a natural disaster

* Climb in the season that is officially designated for climbing.

Learn further about the mountain range and look for any natural disasters that have occurred previously. Make sure that you're aware of the risks and follow the appropriate steps.

Know the mechanism to warn. Be sure to know the significance of warnings in the event that there are warning mechanisms for early detection operating. It is also important to be aware of what to do if the alarm sounds.

What do you do if you are trapped during a natural catastrophe

* Make sure to stay in groups. Be aware of your fellow members' safety and make it simple so that emergency service personnel can locate you.

* To indicate assistance, make loud sounds such as whistles or lighter bits of clothing.

* To assist someone else to keep from taking unnecessary risk. A wounded or injured person is not what any person would like to happen.

3. The Fauna

What is the trigger for animals to come into contact with you?

* In areas in which human activity is low it is a threat to wildlife's ecosystem.

* They could attract animals if you haven't stored your food properly or dispose of your trash.

* You're carrying objects that have a strong scent. Certain strong scents could draw animals.

If you are a witness to wildlife, you will see?

* You may be assaulted by animals afraid or scared.

* Spiders, poisonous snakes and other insects could cause you to be bit or stung.

* Wildlife could steal your food and/or damage your possessions.

How can you avoid encounters with wildlife?

Create noises that can be noisy (in the manner that is considerate rather than blasting the music to the max). If you're climbing in areas where there is a bear population the bear bell is a very popular accessory. A loud walk can scare reptiles and birds away as well.

Make sure you properly keep your food in a safe place. To prevent the smell from entering the zip lock and airtight containers.

• Properly dispose of your trash. Food waste that is left around is similar to leaving your pets with breadcrumbs.

* Sprays are used to kill bugs.

• Stop wearing bright sparkling, flowery clothing that could draw wasps and bees.

What should you do if you are confronted by wildlife:

Don't even approach them. Do not make them feel scared. Move away gently and gently.

* Do not feed wildlife in any way. Also, don't feed any animals that appear innocent and friendly, such as squirrels or deer. Once they've become accustomed of being offered food by humans who feed them, they'll seek out any human for food. They won't refuse to accept a no!

When possible, you should flee and preferably to a safer place If you feel that you're in danger. It is important to make loud sounds if you think that you cannot beat them. You could be able to make yourself appear higher by standing straight and picking massive stones or sticks. Hire your reference. Climbers who aren't experienced can still engage guides. If you are taking on more challenging climbing routes, even experienced climbers can enlist an instructor.

2.2 Why do you think it is more risky to fall down from a mountain?

My wife and me enjoy rock climbing. There are mountains of various kinds. Smaller mountains such as Crowder Mountain in close proximity to Charlotte bigger mountains such as Mt. Washington as well as Mt. Katahdin located in the Northeast and many other powerful mountains in the west, like Mt. Whitney, Border Hill, and Mt. Rainier, which we hope to see eventually. We're awestruck by challenges. are awestruck by snow, we enjoy the thrill of new adventures, learning new things and we love high the altitude. We hear things like "Good luck on your way to the top" or "I would like to see you make it to the top," as well as "send me a photo from the top" when your family members and friends know we're in the process of preparing for an altitude climb.

Although the vibe is friendly and appreciated, reaching the top is the main goal. We're trying to reach the summit. We wouldn't make it if it weren't because of the distinct sense of pride when you're at the top of one of the most beautiful peaks of the United States... even when everything is beneath you, and that includes clouds frequently. However, the ultimate goal is to return down the mountain safely. The climb to the top may be difficult, but many of the biggest dangers occur during descent. Always ask your guide about climbing. They'll inform you that climbing up to the top is not mandatory but it's essential to go down!

What are these major threats? Most likely, you're exhausted from your trek. You've exhausted numerous sets of muscles to make it to. At the top you might have felt the impact of the thinner air. Couple it with the steepness of the descent and you've got a perfect way to cause damage due to falling or excessive use of muscles. A majority of the descent into higher elevations is below the tree line" which indicates that the elements aren't protected. If you're not cautious you may be susceptible to storms in the afternoon , or in certain circumstances afternoon, snow and ice melting.

What happens to services such as food and water? If there was too much consumed during the climb it might not be enough to make it all the descent. There are many sources I can share with you about sharing drinks with those who were dehydrated. The climb was not timed correctly by a lot of climbers, which means that they started late in the morning or getting too long to the top. This can cause some of the descents to be done in darkness or, even more so, some are forced to stay unintentionally sleeping at the top of the hill. A lot of climbers have had their work cut out for them by trying to descend in such a way that they try to take shortcuts, but get stuck.

What does this affect your financial planning and retirement plan specifically? Professionals from our industry and certain families would prefer to invest more of their energy advancing to the point at which they can retire, or so it seems reaching the top. Pay attention to T.V. advertisements: the one titled "What's your number" is one that comes out of your head. It's not a bad thing, it's important to save and work to reach a level that you are able to sustain your quality of life after retirement However, your task isn't done there. I cannot tell you how many times I've heard people say "I'm very happy that I reached retirement, and now all the work is done." Imagine the expression of sadness when I tell them my duties are about to grow for them as their counselor.

On the path to retirement, the biggest threats aren't perceived. Saving, working and spending are all you do. You'll certainly not be short of cash if you have to miss a couple of months of work because of an illness. There won't be any discomfort during your working years if you're insufficiently investing. It's unlikely that you will feel the difference while working in a way that you do not pay the most attention to your savings plan for one or two years. It is possible to be behind or use a significant amount of money, or fail to complete a task but still get all the way to the summit. It's like climbing up to the top. However, it will affect your performance when you come down!

The goal is to reach retirement, and to ensure that you can retire easily without running out of money. Yes what you do in your work life can affect your goal however your actions in retirement will have a greater impact. You're bound to be exhausted once you reach the top. Tired of living, spending on investments, and worrying. You'll want to have a relaxing retirement, but be cautious not to lose focus. When you're down, be aware. Ask someone who is running out of money and is forced to leave their home the last days of their life with their children or rely to Medicaid. It's nearly the same as having to sleep without water, food or shelter in a mountain with the temperature at 20 degrees. Perhaps even more than that, it could be more than one night in your scenario.

What are the possible issues after retirement that can fail? It is easy to lose focus when you feel exhausted or distracted. You think that you can save in the same way that you did when you first came to retirement. You spend too much money, but you don't realize that you must reduce your home's size or you do not have a plan to handle the years when the market is not performing well and you are facing unexpected medical expenses; children parents, grandchildren, or children eat up your financial resources; the risk list is endless.

"I would like to think that I've got your attention and have increased your viewpoint so that you're anxious about the importance of focusing on how to get down safely. What else should you do? Find a system that you can employ to address the problem each year. This isn't a strategy to go down the mountain one time and then forget about it. It continues all the way up and to the bottom. It continues until retirement and beyond in line with the retirement schedule. Find a wealth guide in the event that you do not have a proven method. My wife and I aren't too hesitant to hire guides to help us climb the steep slopes. With Second Half Strategies, we

Our expertise is in this type of planning because reaching and surviving retirement is one of our clients' biggest objectives.

2.3 Is the mountaineering activity the most risky?

The popularity of this sport and the growing practice globally also mean more exposure for the public in the field of rock climbing. When accidents happen it is more well-known to the public about them, especially when they involve celebrities. If these accidents occur in the public eye, all the public can be aware of is that it's risky and risky business's in the final. The actual cause of the incident is likely to go unnoticed in these situations. This is often blamed on the poor judgement or inattention of the climber's own human mistake. This could be due to an overestimation of their abilities or inadequate use of the equipment.

The dangers of climbing rocks are numerous. Many more activities and events that have been played in the past could be accomplished. For example I was afraid of skating for many years as I feared I'd fall and someone else would be able to pass me in a hurry and slice my finger off with their shoe blade. Silly, right? Not. A database from Hospital-data.com provides a total of 891 or so injuries that resulted in finger lacerations during ice skating across the U.S. in 2010. Not a lot If the real incidents are counted. But plenty.

Insofar as climbing is related, I have met several people who think football is more risky than climbing on rocks.

And then when? That's it. In 2006 in the U.S., 4,600,000 people were mountain climbers, in accordance with the National Protection Board, and 3,875 people were injured. This is less than a fraction 0.1. 455,193 of the 17800,000 players who played football were injured during the same year. That represents 2.56 percent. The figures also state that 2014 saw the highest amount of injuries related to climbing mountains, which was 5,395, and we could easily assume that the number of people taking part in this activity has increased. However, Statista.com says that in 2016there were 7.7 million people participated with U.S. climbing events, increasing from 6.6 million in 2007. and for a) very low number of injuries.

A report released in Sports Medicine in 2010, entitled Assessment of Accident and Fatality Risks Rock and Ice climbing, claims that climbing sports have an lower rate of injuries than other sports like sailing, football or soccer. Indoor climbing was the sport with the lowest number of injuries, and had no deaths per 1,000 hours of involvement. In the same way, other climbing disciplines have a lower percentage of injuries than the other sports, and an extremely low level of severity. Most injuries mentioned in studies on rock climbing comprise the upper limbs and especially the fingers, and typically occur as a result of excessive use. There is the possibility of death, especially when it comes to alpine climbing and ice climbing however it's a different story as you will read about.

Here's the exact definition of does it mean to scale rock?

In short, according to Wikipedia the climbers can climb up, down or over artificial or natural wall formations or rock walls when climbing rocks. The objective is to get to without falling the top or the end of a particular point on traditionally established routes. Participants must either complete the route in the least possible time in climbing competitions or make it to the top in a route that is becoming more challenging.

However, "climbing" refers to a concept that covers various things associated with it. It is also known as climbing (rope not climbing to low elevations) as well as sport climbing (mostly lead covered by bolts that is not a risk for the user) and speed-climbing (climbing as fast as you can on a 15-meter-high wall using strict holds arrangements) multi-pitch climbing (longer routes on adventure terrain) Traditional climbing (no established safety measures when climbing) assist climbing (going up using the help of specially-designed equipment) climbing, alpine and ice climbing and many variations of. Indoor (on artificial rock constructions) as well as outdoor climbs is possible. There are many factors that can contribute to the danger based on what you've chosen. But, most importantly you have the freedom of human beings and openness, which can make a difference in the absence of pain.

From where did CLIMBING ROCK get its name?

It is generally accepted that rock climbing began in the final part of the 18th century and was found in 3 areas of Europe within Saxony, Germany, in the northern part of England and in the north of England, which includes Peak as well as Lake Districts, and the Dolomites in Italy. The sport of rock climbing evolved from an alpine necessity into a sport of its own at the beginning of the 20th century. In the 1920s it was the U.S. saw European climbing techniques spreading across the globe. In the years following the conflict, Yosemite Valley, California became the biggest climbing area of the time. In the case of climbing indoors, at the University of Leeds, the first climbing wall that was publically accessible was built in England in the early 1960s. It was intended to function as a learning area for outdoor climbers.

What are the main elements involved in climbing rocks?

Typically, such setups and special safety devices are needed. Also, it requires another person to join up with. This, in conjunction and mental discipline demands physical and mental endurance as well as agility, endurance, and balance. It requires transparency, maturity of thought, and the ability to search easily and understand the context and make the right decisions when it comes to more advanced activities.

Outside INDOOR VERSUS CLIMBING

There are real risks and physical dangers in outdoor climbing including unpredictable consistency of ice and rock and weather conditions that are unpredictable and equipment that could harm you if used them properly (ice axes) difficult approaches, more physical and mental stress. External environmental elements in mountaineering, like crevasses, avalanches and other altitude-related illnesses, could directly lead to accidents or even deaths. If you are able to practice alpine climbing or rescue methods with a good understanding of local terrain, taking care with adjustment or paying careful attention to the reactions of your body's response to altitude and conditions, they can be avoided or effectively controlled.

Contrary to this, risks from external and objective sources are considerably reduced for sports and indoor climbing However, there is the possibility of serious injury. Because of their skills and experience, the majority of climbers can manage these dangers and avoid serious injury. Many small and major events are held each year across the U.S. and around the world, such as world championships, and possibly the next Olympics in Tokyo that shouldn't be considered dangerous athletic activities. Training and indoor climbing and events.

Let's see what you can guess. There is no defined definition of a 'high-risk' sport, and that's why it was determined to be either arbitrarily defined or determined by the definition that defines climbers as one. Also, only a handful of sports are not considered being high-risk such as mountain biking, football handball soccer (as as a touch sport) or horse riding as per the current definitions (because of the risk of a fatal accident).

If you look around the danger, there's nothing more dangerous than attending an evening football game on a Friday night. Go ahead, give it a go climbing the rock and enjoy the thrills. But make sure that you are able to master the basics from knowledgeable and well-experienced people. They will teach you the best strategies and, perhaps most importantly the best way to utilize the tools correctly in a healthy environment, both physical and social. The enjoyment is the most important. Enjoy yourself. Climbing has a lot of advantages, and is a social activity.

2.4 The reason for why the majority of climbers dying?

It was thought that climbing Mount Everest with or without oxygen would be physically impossible. Hillary as well as Tenzing showed in 1953 it's feasible to climb the mountain without oxygen. Messner and Habeler proved that it was feasible without oxygen as of 1978. Today, we have a better knowledge of acclimatization techniques, modern climbing equipment, and established routes that have fixed lines that lead climbers to the summit however, the top of Everest is not changing. The cylinders are much smaller than those that ascend by oxygen.

Thus, it is natural that climbing Everest could have been an easier task. But, in the year 2000, the unofficial count of bodies for Mount Everest had reached 15 which is the highest since the tragic event in 1996, when 16 people perished, and eight of them in the course of one night, following an unplanned storm. A study of Mount Everest death rate between the years 1980 and 2002 revealed that it was not improving in the past and there was a death per ten ascends. If you reach the summit, the shocking truth is that you're almost a one per 20 chance of getting back down. So, why are so many deaths at the top of Mount Everest? In particular, how is it possible to get the number of deaths to a minimum?

Fatigue and injuries are the main causes of those who die while climbing Mount Everest. However, a significant portion of climbers die due to illnesses related to altitude, including those suffering from high-altitude cerebral swelling (HACE) as well as high altitude pulmonary edema are also suffering from (HAPE). The reason for death is typically confirmed by a co-climber and, as such, is not 100% certain. The illness of altitude could also have contributed to the death of a climber and fatigue-related deaths.

I was stunned by the severity of illness caused by altitude as well as the lack of information of those who attempted Everest. Two high altitude pulmonary edema cases as well as one instance of high altitude cerebral edema during my expedition of only 15 individuals, which is significantly more than the 1-3 percent rate forecast. The good news is that all of these patients have recovered completely.

We were able to assist people suffering from high altitude pulmonary Edema, which was at 7000m, during our summit ascent however, we also crossed the bodies of four climbers that were less fortunate on the mountain. We came across the final body of an Frenchman two days earlier, who had made it to the top but was exhausted to continue his descent. His friend was able to help him descend the mountain, but in vain however, in just six hours they had only climbed 50 meters and he was forced to leave his friend.

Many believe that the large number of novice climbers paying huge sums of money for the privilege of climbing Everest is a factor in the rising number of deaths. However, every climber I know who passed away this year experienced the thrill of climbing to 8000 feet. I believe that climbers don't go above their capacity, but rather over their capabilities to climb elevation. Unfortunately that, if you don't climb Everest the climb is inconceivable to experience the experience of climb above Camp 3 (8300 meters). It is a fact that climbers rarely know what their capabilities will be when they reach 8300 meters.

There is a shift in the sense of perception due to cerebral edema. Lincoln Hall, a climber who attempted to climb Everest this year, who suffered cerebral edema at high altitude on the descent from the top, illustrates this. After being declared dead, a different group of climbers discovered him later that day. He was convinced that he was aboard a sailing vessel. He also hopped on the radio and started planning the rescue, unaware that the rescue wasn't really intended for him.

Are there milder forms of this disorientation which can allow climbers to fool themselves into thinking to believe that they are able to climb to the top before going down? It is my opinion that once we reach the top, we all suffer from cerebral and pulmonary edema. It is likely it's just an issue of time before we fall victim to it. When climbing climbers must focus less on the climb as much about the health of their. It doesn't matter what the problem such as HAPE, HACE or simply fatigue, the result is the same. The climber will begin to climb at a slower pace. Your ascent rate should be less than 1-1.5 hours for every 100m. This indicates that something is not right If you're not on time and the chances of not making it to the top of the mountain have been significantly increased. When the summit is in view this tip is often ignored.

"When I was required to go to the French consulate in Kathmandu to confirm the Frenchman's death and the consul was shaking his head. He was not an expert on climbing or an altitude expert that I have heard of. He then declared, "He did not hit the top at 12.30 which is a 14-hour climb that is too long. It took him for so long to get to the top. All the reports we receive from people who died on the mountain, it's the same thing. it's the same thingit's the same thing.

Chapter 16: What Makes Climbing Mountains Costly?

The most difficult difficulty for an explorer is mountaineering at high altitude, which involves mixing expedition-grade climbing with high altitude dangerous cliffs, dangerous rock ledges, and jaw-dropping views. But it's an excellent price as well.

The cost can quickly escalate into thousands of dollars, from preparing for a major climb, to paying for an excursion to an isolated mountain range. Be patient, however and don't waste your hard-earned cash You can enjoy the excitement of climbing. Here are some suggestions to get you going.

Guidance, knowledge and guidance

Join the club

This is your first stop at your local mountain club. They are present in all countries, and offer instruction, guidance and equipment rental, as well as discounts, and forums in which you can seek assistance, get together and even share the cost of your next adventure.

Cut corners from books

It's all about awareness and on books that are brand new it's not necessary to buy a new one. Older editions can are available on Amazon for a low price. For beginners, you can buy Freedom of the Hills, the 'Mountaineering Guide and look up for nearby online tools to get practical tips for those who are looking to refresh their knowledge on a particular route.

Find out the credentials yourself

In taking classes to be accredited by the government, you can eliminate guides completely saving thousands. Make sure to pick an adventure that you are able to accept and know the moment to back off. The risk of pushing yourself beyond your capabilities is nearly as dangerous with no training as mountain climbing.

Take a trip to the places where guides are less expensive,

Guidebooks can be expensive If you're in need of one, look for the area that is less expensive. There are low-cost guides that are safe for Asia or South America, but they can also be a place where fraud is a common occurrence So, make sure you verify the credentials of their guides. When they're available, it might be worth it to purchase an accredited IFMGA guide.

Socializing with climbers

Find the closest climbing spot until you reach the place you'd like to go and learn about the people who are there. An option to hire a climber could be to hire someone who is knowledgeable of the area.

On-line Search Free Maps

It is possible that you do not need to pay for O.S. charts. For central mountain ranges, websites like Wander map provide routes for free, however, should they not be accurate enough, you should purchase a high-quality route map. When the conditions are nice visual feedback can be useful. Print photos too.

Finding the perfect spot

Stay in close proximity to your home

Find a map and talk with local guides to locate areas that you've never known about if you are in or close to the great outdoors. For Class 3 and 4 routes, take a look at Summit Post; these are technically challenging, but not as equipment-intensive, meaning you don't need to spend too much in all the equipment.

Take care to select a pad.

If you're in the business and renting your house out to pay for the long haul just end your rental and move towards the mountains, so why should you not? If you purchase a home and want to swap houses in a mountain city with other people. Consider couch surfing, buy a quality tent and search for campsites that are free for shorter trips, or purchase an used car and sleep in the back seat for trips that are shorter.

Pay for travel expenses with in-country investments

A single flight cost could make you turn away from an insignificant location however, once you are there, you must be aware of the local cost. If you're planning to become an avid mountaineer for some time it is possible to save 10-20 euros per day could be enough to pay for the ticket.

Get rid of the big names and go to places that are less expensive.

It is a popular activity to climb peaks like Mount Kilimanjaro and Aconcagua comes with higher prices, and not only for guidance as well as for lodging food, accommodation, and more, so steer off. Peru can be reasonably priced in addition, the Cordillera Blanca is beautiful around Huaraz. In Himachal Pradesh, or Ladakh which has low peak prices and mountains as high as 5,500 meters, Northern India is comparatively affordable and easy to reach and offers an excellent introduction to the Himalayas. Kyrgyzstan is also a budget however stunning place once you reach it.

Secret fees Beware

If you're going to a foreign country Do not compromise on insurance. Also, don't forget vaccinations and permits however, make use of price comparison sites to find the most affordable expert-level cover plan.

Utilize your miles.

Find frequent flier miles on business trips if you travel to work and take them to have fun. In most cases, it's better when traveling in this part of the U.S. to use them within the state. Beware of school holidays, avoid flying during between week days, and join an online tracking of travel prices to determine the most affordable airfares if you don't have miles.

Make use of human fuel, a fleet of vehicles or a cheaper mode of transport.

It's an enormous cost to travel to the mountains. However, you can save money by hiking or riding in the event that there is time, and the resources. To cut down on fuel costs or gas, rent a car with a friend if you must drive. Book early and secure specific time-specific tickets when traveling via train.

Services, clothing and food

You can borrow the equipment, or sell it to transfer it to another person.

It can be expensive to wear armor and budgets shouldn't be cut. If you're unable to purchase it, you can borrow quality items, and when you do have the money to buy it, take note of the possibility you took and give it to someone who wants to become a mountaineer. Check out the emblem for the UIAA to ensure it's not outdated.

Take a look at eBay for car boot sales, eBay as well as Craigslist.

Find bargain stores where people sell old equipment even if you're not able to take it home. Car boot sales can be a great source of inexpensive equipment in mountain regions particularly if you are able to repair damaged items, such as torn seams. But, make sure it's well-maintained. It's your life.

Be sure to spend the money on the correct clothes

The two layers aren't identical. Consider why you'll need it in the first place and whether it's a high-tech item prior to purchasing it. Because this is your first layer of protection, spend more on outerwear , such as jackets and salopettes. Also, there are a variety of good, cheaper base layers. Be sure to check your wardrobe prior to leaving if you are in a cold climate. Don't spend excessively unless, if your clothing is wet and you're underwear will be the sole item you'll need to change.

Do not make transactions last minute.

Be prepared before you go out, and give yourself the time to search for the product you require at the lowest price or for free from a friend.

"Be "last year, so

There is no need to make second-hand purchases. Look for bargains towards the closing of the season to determine what was the most popular item this year or before , and then purchase it up until the new batch of products is introduced with huge discounts.

For the length, carry food.

It's much more convenient to purchase groceries in bulk rather than buy things on the go So, buy it in the bulk. You should plan your diet well to increase the amount of nutrients you consume, decrease the weight and eliminate food waste. Noodles are the best friend of climbers, they are inexpensive easy to store and very light, but nutritious and delicious.

Multi-tasking of services

For the purposes they're intended for, they don't require to be used. An avalanche detector could include a tent rod hiking poles could be used as canoe paddles or frames with a bivvy bag or garbage bag to create an umbrella for rain Iodine tablets are able to purify water, but they also disinfect wounds. Bandages and tape could patch devices, as can the user and may be used as gloves that you can make.

Purchase gear in phases

It's not necessary to immediately have all the equipment and equipment, so you can spread costs to ease the burden. A basic layering scheme of clothes along with good boots, an outdoor stove and tent will suffice for backpacking when you're getting started. Include a scrambling helmet and then rope, a belt and climbing equipment to give you professional-grade training. Also, for snowy routes, you should add sturdy boots, crampons, and cold-weather clothes.

4.1 What is an Mount Everest climbing permit cost?

In becoming the youngest person ever to climb Mount Everest, the highest mountain above sea level Tseten Sherpa is a 9 year old boy from Nepal hopes to set a new world record. The most difficult task may not be the summit at 29,035 feet (8850 meters) and climbing the summit of the mountain has a an expensive price.

What is the reason why it cost so excessively?

Dennis Broad well, the proprietor of Mountain Gurus, a business that offers mountain treks with a guide up to Mount Everest, said The permit is issued per trip that has between seven and 10 people on each permit.' "That means the price amounts to about $10,000 per person."

The cost is $25,000 if an individual who is a mountaineer would like to buy an individual permit. The money collected for the permit from the Nepalese government is used to ensure that Mount Everest remains in pristine condition and that the locals believe it is sacred. A group comprising 20 Sherpa climbers trekked up to The "death region" in the mountains (26,000 metres above sea-level or higher) in April of this year to clear the debris left from previous expeditions.

While it could appear to be the cost of a guided tour as well as lodging for the price is part of the license, in reality it really includes the cost for entry into the mountain. It is bought in order to get an official certificate of Nepal's Government of Nepal confirming their accomplishment if they are able to reach the summit.

The permit also grants the climbers legal authority to climb Mount Everest, so that the Nepalese authorities are able to evacuate climbers in event in an emergency. If you don't have a permit for the summit However, they aren't in luck because they aren't legally permitted to be on the peak and thus would not be considered to be a valid candidate for.

The price of the permit goes towards the cost of liaison officers who watch over the trail at different campsites. They monitor the use of communications equipment by climbers, assist climbers get forecasts for weather and make sure that climbers adhere to the strict climbing schedule since climbing is not permitted after 6 after 6 pm in the mountains.

"The total cost of climbing Mount Everest is overwhelming even without the permit cost and the "optional" cost of round-trip trips, mountaineering guides and tents, oxygen tanks and communications equipment easily exceeding the figure of $200,000 as per the U.S. Administration of Federal Aviation.

Broad well-told Life's Little Mysteries "A bottles of oxygen will cost between $300 and $400 and every person should carry around 5 or 6 bottles throughout an adventure." "That's approximately two grand to buy oxygen. Anyone contemplating a serious climb of Mount Everest are well aware of the amount it's going to cost."

However, even the event that Tseten Sherpa manages to bring the resources together, it's likely that there's a decent possibility that the whole thing will not be worth it. In June an act that barred those under 18 years old from mountain climbing dangerous mountain was adopted in the China Tibet Mountaineering Association, who oversees all mountaineering trips within China-controlled Tibet. To be able to climb the Nepali side climbers must be 16 years old.

4.2 What's the cost of cost the Everest 2020 climb cost?

The thing that really awes those who aren't a part of the mountaineering world is how much it will cost when I talk about the preparation and time required for a climb to Everest. Even for experienced mountaineers it's not uncommon to experience a little "sticker surprise" when estimating the cost of an Everest climb, especially since the cost of climbing Everest continues to increase each year.

Thankfully, our friend Alan Arnette still does a excellent job keeping track of price increases and dividing in his annual blog post where the money will go. Just a few days ago, Alan posted the figures prior to the start of the spring 2020 season, referring again to the old question of "how much will the cost of climbing Everest?" "

How much will the climb to Mount Everest cost?

The cost for an Everest adventure is likely to rise by 2020, which is the case over the last few years. Alan says that at the lower price, climbers could spend around $30,000 while on the higher end it could cost up to $160,000. This year, the average person will pay around $45,000, which is an increase only a little compared to last year's.

The truth is that China recently raised the cost of a permit to climb to the summit from the North Side, going from $9950 up to an astounding $15,800 is a part of the price increase. Nepal is expected to follow suit and increase the cost of permits too, but it hasn't yet happened at the time of this time of writing.

In addition, there is financing in Nepal to help maximize the overall cost of an expedition. If more and more Nepali guide firms emerge locally, locals have a stake in ensuring they are given a fair amount of compensation. In the wake of this, authorities are looking at the possibility of requiring trips to each have the minimum of $35,000, and setting the price floor.

It isn't expected to affect the costs of this year's expedition, however it could be a factor in the near future.

Alan will also look at the past year to look at patterns and other factors that are a result of his normal level of detail-orientedness followed by a wrap with a detailed spreadsheet that is broken into different categories.

The Cost of Overcrowding

Arnette explains the story of a turbulent year for the mountain, with significant crowding in the South Side, long queues at the top, and a number of deaths that could be prevented. This calls for a thorough analysis of the way that events from 2019 affect the 2020 climbing season.

The whole thing hangs like a dark cloud over 2020 season. The same scenario could be repeated for the next spring could turn out to be devastating.

How Much Does it Cost to climb Mount Everest?

In 2020, the median cost of an position on an commercial Everest team, which could be out of Tibet and Nepal. A cost of about US$20,000 for an easy attempt to climb Everest can be planned. Private climbs of Futenbach's "signature expedition" has a pricey cost of around US$200,000 at the top of the range.

The simple option is ideal for mountaineers with vast experience over 8,000m and who are in the region that is known as the death zone for solo climbing operations, expedition preparation, and operation.

It is estimated that the Furtenbach team that ascends from Tibet is priced at US$60,900 in the higher price point. The cost of being in the Alpenglow U.S. team is $85,000. The "private climbing alternative" of IMG and includes for every climber an individual western guide, includes an all-in cost of US$118,000. For the RMI team the private climbing option will cost you US$135,000. The most expensive package can be found at $200,000 with Furtenbach's "signature expedition" with an individual guide and professionally trained Sherpas and pre-acclimatization. There are also unlimited oxygen tanks food and fitness plans and many other facilities.

As a rule the more programmers are provided, the greater the price, but this statement shouldn't be taken as a guarantee. These additional programmers can include:

A higher proportion of western guides who have had previous experience

* Extra assistance from the Sherpa

* Extra oxygen bottles that can be used to achieve higher flow rates

* Clear demands for diets

* Bigger tents for Base Camp

* Contact us for more information.

* The provision of tents for pre-acclimatization to be used for six weeks prior to the departure.

Expedition 2021 on Everest

With years of experience, well-prepared and a keen eye Our Everest expedition schedule is designed to ensure maximum days of the journey, with the highest quality of service and a mighty group of guides. We offer trips with top the highest level of protection and assistance. In the base camp and Camp 2, we provide additional oxygen and support, and offer an easy logistical support.

Namche Bazar, Tengboche, Dingboche, Lobuche, Gorekshep and then Everest base camp. These are all followed by the usual trekking route until Everest Base Camp. Relax and organize yourself before we begin the actual climb when we arrive to Base Camp.

The base camp is where, where ice seracs from Lower Khumbu Glacier to check climbers equipment, and also to learn methods for rescue and climbing. training sessions will be held. Instead of the regular Khumbu Icefall rotations, you could also climb Lobuche East as part of your climbing acclimatization.

A single of the more exciting treks of 6000m in the Everest region includes Lobuche East. To be used for Everest Expeditions, Lobuche east climb is a fantastic training base. This is exactly what we'll do in Highland Expeditions as well. To help you relax you'll be climbing Lobuche east in your high altitude boots and other gear. This mountain isn't just an exciting opportunity for a break, but also is a major component of the acclimatization phase that helps participants refresh and improve their mountain-based skills prior to heading towards Everest.

Climbing the East Peak of Lobuche prior to climbing the Everest climb will not only aid in the process of acclimatization, but also for the rotation of climbing camps at higher elevations, the climbers do not have to trek through The Khumbu Icefall many times. We return to our base camp following the climb. Afterwards, taking a look at a lucky date as per the Tibetan calendar, we organize a traditional Sherpa puja ceremony to ask for the blessings needed for an enjoyable Everest Climb.

The rotation of the higher camps passing through the notorious Khumbu Icefall begins with the second acclimatization phase. The four centers are set up over our base camp. At the top of the icefall Camp2 (6,400m/21,000ft) is located Western Cwm, which will be our Advanced Base Camp, we are making plans for Camp1 (5,900m/19,500ft). On the summit of the circus, on Lhotse Face, we will establish Camp 3 (7,300m/23,700ft). Before reaching the top, Camp 4 (7,900m/25,912ft) will be the last camp. Camp 4 will be moved into South Col.

To acclimatize, be aware that during the duration of the exploration phase, this program for acclimatization will differ because each climber adjusts to altitude in a different way. According to your particular needs, your leader will suggest the best option for you. Our acclimatization schedule is comprised of Camp 2 overnight and the Lhotse Face/Camp 3 sign. Once this has been completed and we wait until the right weather conditions that will allow the summit attempt, we rest and rest on the ground. To make it a simple climbing experience, oxygen tanks should be utilized following Camp 3. To ensure that the flow is full the climbers are provided the oxygen bottles for eight days. We'll reach South Summit from Camp 4. South Summit from Camp 4 by following the south-east ridge. From where we'll head towards Hillary Step before climbing to the summit.

We're making sure that they're relaxed and knowledgeable. In this section, the majority of our guides are born and have relatives in different areas of the areas in where the were raised. In the course of uncertain adventure, where something could occur, we know local workers are an essential component. We ensure the Highland Expeditions that our mountain team are highly motivated and do not make a mistake.

Small business with years of experience at altitudes.

Everest in History

Highland Expeditions is a fully licensed and registered business located in the Himalayas which offers high altitude expeditions. Since the year 1992, folks who manage this company have been leading high-altitude trips, and we're extremely proud to offer customized trips to Mt. Everest with the top priority of security and operational.

With the help of our experienced Sherpa guide, we operate an unison group of climbers who have all reached the summit of Everest. We limit ourselves to eight climbers as a group and offer an 1:1 Sherpa guide-to-customer ratio, with oxygen support and easy logistics arrangements for the Nepali IAGM/UIAGM Expedition Leader.

Chapter 17: What Are The Benefits From Climbing Mountains?

The main benefits of physical fitness and health are

You will not only (consistently) develop tremendous strength and endurance the climb however, you'll discover that your diet is becoming better. In the region of the alpine, McDonald's are not readily accessible (thank for the convenience!) So, you'll be required to pack your lunches and snacks.

It is also evident that unhealthy food choices will not properly provide you with energy. A healthy diet is essential for the physical demands of climbing and hiking. The altitude helps your lungs to be stronger and, with each day you go hiking and climb, the effort becomes smaller and less. In the natural world, there's much to learn from your exercises.

It is possible to see places that are seldom visited by people.

We all have seen images of these spots and we all want to visit these locations but the work required to access these locations takes many of us out from the crowd. Time and energy for climbing a mountain that's an amazing day-long hike to high altitude can be a lot of a challenge for some.

You can rest at ease knowing that you're one of the lucky ones to reach the summit once you reach the top and revel in the beauty and uniqueness of this panoramic view. It's a good thing that when you're at the summit of an mountain, you're sure to see the most amazing views (unless it's a cloudy day or a smokey day).

You'll meet some amazing people that you could call friends

Climbers and Hikers are an amazing collection of people. There are a few commonalities among them: all are optimistic they are all solid and confident and they all are content. One of the most effective ways to find hiking companions will include meeting people via hiking clubs, alpine groups, and social media.

The best thing about walking is that we have the same goal of getting to the summit of the mountain and to take in an exercise session and enjoying the beauty of nature. So, long-lasting friendships are made since you typically spend a great deal of time together. Also, you get to meet them in some of the most stunning places that can bring people together in different ways.

In the end, you'll know why the mountains call and that you need to leave.

The mountains are so majestic They seem to have a magical aura. Maybe it's because they're so risky or perhaps it's due to the fact that they feel small. They'll even call you even when you're not even climbing up them.

If you are lucky, you're with them, everything in your life are dissolved or your life slows down slightly. All I can tell you is that you'll be compelled to return after being surrounded by them or climbing on them.

The climb up a mountain will demonstrate the patience, determination and respect.

The furthest thing from being easy is climbing the top of a mountain. The most exhausting, and the most demanding thing you can will encounter is the long hours of constant vertical climbing. Additionally, you'll be examined not just for health issues, as well as for psychological issues.

The greatest of your mental abilities can be honed through a variety of uncovered and difficult climbing, as well as the search for paths. The old saying that tells you to "take one piece at a time and consider the whole mountain" is something you'll learn to take note of. You'll be taught to never give up , knowing that the effort is worth the rewards.

It could take a few months, days, and hours to climb however, it will take you a while, but you will succeed in climbing. You'll know what there is to be excited about when you've completed it. It's about achieving an objective, achieving an ambition and discovering that anything you set your thoughts to is accomplished. It's a thrilling feeling nobody can accurately describe and that you must observe.

These will help you remember of why we desire that the planet be saved.

You'll want to protect them once you see what the unexplored places are. Human intervention and precise cutting is the most difficult option for you to do in any of these breathtaking areas. In the end, you may realize the fact that in national parks, there are a lot of rules and that is why you are happy to have these guidelines.

The most beautiful areas can turn into tourist hotspots so the best way to let other people appreciate these spots is to ensure they are preserved. You'll appreciate what we are able to enjoy a bit more when you climb the mountains. To make a difference in every way that I can I've found that I reuse less, recycle more and reuse more products.

They will show you how to be optimistic,

It's a sure way to be disappointed if feel apprehensive about climbing the mountain. It isn't helpful to believe that you aren't capable of it or that it's hard in any way. If you're confident, you will continue striving even though it's impossible right now.

I keep reminding myself that in order to finish this climb I need to make a 100% commitment. If you aren't convinced that you'll be able to conquer a mountain, you'll never be able to climb it. You are more capable than you think you'll be because all you need to do is believe in yourself, be confident in yourself and take slowly, bite by bite and in no time you'll reach the highest point.

They will share with you the little pleasures of life that you will love.

Six hours of gruelling horizontal heat and you rest for a moment by the water. It's going to be the most refreshing water you've ever had the pleasure of tasting. We often forget about the small things we overlook in our lives, like water.

You'll know how cold the wind can create and how vital small things are when they're not around at the top, but you've forgotten to pack your coat. We are taught to be well-prepared and enjoy things that are comfortable such as not having to sleep in cold temperatures on hard rocks as an example.

They will teach you about the transition process and prepare you for the inevitable changes.

You must be aware that the weather can change quickly If you've ever spent in the mountains, which is why organizing yourself is vital. Each mountain is unique which means you must change your route frequently.

There is only one path up a slope and often, there are alternative routes or obstacles in the path. Mountains can show you that things aren't always as they seem and, to make the situation, you must try a different strategy.

A mountain can inform you.

I am still convinced that each mountain I have climbed has taught me a important lesson at minimum. I found out from a rainy climb that cameras aren't waterproof! Another climb has taught me to make sure I am prepared to be ready for the road (more research.). When you learn something, regardless of whether they advise you to carry an umbrella in case you need to stay up all night or tell you that the right shoes are necessary. Mountain climbing could be the most enjoyable and difficult thing you'll ever experience in your life, but you always want more in the end regardless of the outcome.

3.1 What body part is responsible to support mountaineers?

It's a difficult task for most people to climb a mountain, but what happens if the mountain is actually the floor? The idea for mountain climbers is. You alternate pulling one knee towards your chest out of an incline of a plank and then back in taking a step forward each time before "running" on the ground.

While it may sound easy however, the whole body is being exercised by mountain climbers and the heart rate gets increased. It is easy to introduce mountain climbers into the routine of waking up at home or the gym while traveling on a bed in the hotel or even sneak them in when you're in the break room at work. This simple method is ideal for novices, but with some modifications, more experienced exercisers can step it to the next level.

Benefits

Mountain climbers are great for endurance as well as core strength and agility development. Mountain climbers train with a variety of muscles by doing just one workout, it's than a full-body exercise.

Your arms, shoulders, and chest are all working to keep your upper body in balance as your heart stabilizes the rest of your body as you transfer. Your quads also receive an excellent workout as they are the main movement. Since it's a cardio exercise, you'll get cardiovascular benefits for your heart, as well as burning calories.

Step-by-Step instructions

Try the traditional version of the exercise if you're just beginning:

Take the plank position and ensure that your weight is evenly distributed between your hands and toes.

Hands should sit shoulder width apart, your back straight, your abs engaged and your head in a straight line. Make sure you are in alignment with your posture.

* Move your right leg as deep as you are able toward your mouth.

* Pull one knee away to turn your legs, then put the other knee on top.

* Keep your hips in a low position and move your knees as long and as fast as you can both in and out. Alternate exhalation and inhalation as you move your leg.

Popular Errors

There are several common errors that could make it less effective or even risky especially for climbers on mountain.

On the Toes bouncing

It is not only important to train correctly to boost your performance however, you must also be safe from injuries. To begin, bouncing around on your feet as you perform the exercise is a common error made by beginners when it comes to mountain climbers. It may seem like an exercise that is more strenuous but your core muscles require less effort.

Inability to make your toes contact the floor

Another error you could make, especially in the speed of the workout you are not completing the entire exercise by letting your heels land on the floor as you pull your knees to your chest. If you discover that this is happening to you, you could not benefit from the full benefits of the exercise and be in danger of injury.

Moving Back Your Weight

It's easy for your body to fluctuate back when you aren't experienced enough to do this and your body will end with a down-dog position. Make sure you are balancing the weight with your wrists placed over your shoulders.

Modifications and Variations

To customize the workout to your ability and level Utilize the following Mountain Climber variants.

Do you want to change the way your car is used?

Begin with a less impactful version if you're at a beginning stage.

Mountain Climbers Low-Impact

Your right knee should be brought to your chest as you move from a plank and keep your left foot straight.

As your toes hit the deck, you can bring your right foot to the stage of planning.

Perform the move swiftly by bringing your left leg up to your shoulders again, holding your left leg away from the floor.

Bring your left foot back to the spot where you plank where you can touch the ground using your heels, and then lift your right foot to automatically repeat step 2.

Alternate sides with ease for one minute or for the amount of reps you select.

If you are feeling it necessary to take some weight off your hands, head and shoulders, consider trying an exercise with different mountain climbers. The upper body is lifted up during an exercise or block for this variant. If you're resuming exercise after an injury or working to improve your upper-body capability, this could be beneficial.

Are you up for the Challenge?

Try a more advanced version after you've mastered the basics.

Mountain Climbers Foot-Switch

The foot-switch is instead of sprinting. It's more efficient and gives you the chance to increase the heart rate.

Start by locating a spot on the plank.

Your broad toe should be tapped towards your floor as you pull the right leg upwards.

Make sure you switch your feet, then immediately shift your right foot backwards and your left foot inward.

Repeat the exercise for the desired number of reps or the time you want to use.

Mountain Climbers Sliding

If you own the disc that glides or a towel, and you have a hardwood floor you might want to alter the basic action using the discs or towels.

Set your towel or disc on the board, and when you are in the plank position, position your foot on the board.

Utilizing the non-sliding leg and your upper body to stabilize yourself, gradually begin to perform a simple exercise.

It is evident when you do the quads instead of the simple version as you increase the intensity of the step.

There is a possibility that you have a disorder called diastasisrecti, in which the abdominal muscles are divided, regardless of whether you've just had a baby or had some type of abdominal surgeries.

You'll need to stay clear of this type of core workout until the disorder is fully recovered.

3.2 Does it encourage mountain climbers to shed belly fat?

A few ab exercises that involve the full abdominal area and aerobic exercise include mountain climber abs exercises and its variations. While crunches, sit-ups, planks and other exercises strengthen your muscles and improve your are sound, the exercise associated with the M.T. climber also burns fat. You can eliminate the fat on your tummy for an appealing flat stomach.

The exercise has been proven to build the heart and increase the rate which consumes fat. You must include this fundamental workout into your routine in order to build solid, smooth abs in only a few weeks. There are several variations to help you get greater speed and performance , too.

How do we help mountain climbers be treated better?

In all combinations in all the combinations, this is the essential movement. Start with a position of push-ups. Then you have to press your knees towards your chest. Throughout the exercise you should keep a straight posture that your back lowers. You will then pull you legs to as many inches as you can. Focus on your abdominal muscles. You must feel the way they work.

Different ways to climb rocks

1. Climber Diagonal

This exercise is very similar to the standard one, with only one difference. with the elbows opposite to where the feet are placed. The more you push your knees inwards and the more effective this abdominal workout is. It's great for hips and obliques, to help stabilize and reduce fat.

2. Climber to Spider

This is a specific place and now, you're putting your feet on top of your hands. Put your foot as far forward as you can to get the greatest results. Stretch your leg while it's placed in the reverse position.

3. From Side of Climber

This may be the most difficult one. The knees are brought to the sides of your body, instead of making those knees up straight.

4. Version Cross Body

The routine continues with the standard climb, with the exception that you lift your knees up to an opposite elbow.

Do these two movements three to four times over the course of a session, doing 20 reps for each. You're supposed to complete approximately. 300-400 repeats. Your workout must be vigorous to maximize the fat burning phase, but make sure you properly shape your workout routine. Perform it for 3-4 days per week at the very least.

Mountain climbers can be a fantastic exercise for the entire body. Because you start in a plank position that you are in, you will be working your core. Mountain climbers are an incredibly powerful move that swiftly raises the heart rate, firing every muscle group of the body, such as deltoids, chest abs, oblique's abdominals, quads, hamstrings and hip abductors.

You should reduce your calories consumed or drink to the amount of calories you're able to consume daily to shed belly fat. To achieve this, you have to keep an check on your intake of calories. You should also exercise frequently to burn more calories.

One of the issues that we are concerned about is the reduction of belly fat. It is area of fat around the stomach, which is processed. The excess belly fat can negatively impact your health. Certain serious diseases including high blood sugar or high cholesterol, high blood pressure and various heart-related diseases, could be caused. Thus, melting belly fat is important. You should reduce the amount of calories you consume or simply drink the amount of calories you are able to burn daily to lose belly fat. In order to do this, it is necessary to keep an check on your intake of calories and exercise regularly to burn more calories. A nutritious and healthy diet is also effective in reducing belly fat quickly.

Conclusion

While rock climbing is thought to be very dangerous however, it's an extremely thrilling activity that can push you beyond your limits in both physical and mental terms. It's also an excellent method to visit the stunning locations around the globe and enjoy the great outdoors. So long as you're secure, climbing can enrich your life in numerous ways.

Now you'll be more aware of the equipment you should purchase and how to stay sure to be safe when climbing, the various forms of rock climbing, as well as specific methods to climb safely. As you will notice climbing requires more than strength. It requires planning to conserve energy and endurance and maintain the balance and be in good shape, as well as specific steps to improve reach. There is a huge benefit by using the correct rock climbing methods while developing your muscle strength through practice.

This guide explains a lot of the fundamentals to climbing, however to really advance, you'll need to go out and begin climbing! The more you practice, the better according to the old saying.

The more you practice your movements, the more they will become natural to you. The more you study and analyze ways to perform them as you progress, the more you'll be able to know how to tackle every challenge. The more consistently you exercise and work out, the stronger your muscles, such as the back, shoulders and neck muscles, the in between the elbows and the thighs. It is essential to continue training because it's easy for you to slow down your gains.

Go out and start your climbs! I hope that you've gained many things from this book and can use it to make dramatic gains in your climbing.

www.ingramcontent.com/pod-product-compliance
Lightning Source LLC
Chambersburg PA
CBHW050412120526
44590CB00015B/1938